A Word Shared Between Us

A Word Shared Between Us

Praying in a Time of Exile

Travis O'Brian

RESOURCE *Publications* • Eugene, Oregon

A WORD SHARED BETWEEN US
Praying in a Time of Exile

Copyright © 2022 Travis O'Brian. All rights reserved. Except for brief quotations in critical publications or reviews, no part of this book may be reproduced in any manner without prior written permission from the publisher. Write: Permissions, Wipf and Stock Publishers, 199 W. 8th Ave., Suite 3, Eugene, OR 97401.

Resource Publications
An Imprint of Wipf and Stock Publishers
199 W. 8th Ave., Suite 3
Eugene, OR 97401

www.wipfandstock.com

PAPERBACK ISBN: 978-1-6667-3046-3
HARDCOVER ISBN: 978-1-6667-2204-8
EBOOK ISBN: 978-1-6667-2205-5

JANUARY 7, 2022 9:33 AM

Unless otherwise indicated, scripture quotations are from New Revised Standard Version Bible, copyright © 1989 National Council of the Churches of Christ in the United States of America. Used by permission. All rights reserved worldwide, or from the Revised Standard Version of the Bible copyright © 1946, 1952, and 1971 National Council of the Churches of Christ in the United States of America. Used by permission. All rights reserved worldwide.

I will seek Thee, Lord, by calling on Thee . . .
—ST. AUGUSTINE, *CONFESSIONS*

Contents

Introduction | xi

MARCH 18	Cyril of Jerusalem | 1
MARCH 19	St. Joseph of Nazareth | 3
MARCH 20	Cuthbert, Bishop of Lindisfarne | 5
MARCH 23	Gregory the Illuminator | 7
MARCH 24	Lenten Feria | 9
MARCH 25	The Annunciation of the Lord to the Blessed Virgin Mary | 11
MARCH 26	Lenten Feria | 13
MARCH 27	Charles Henry Brent, Bishop | 15
MARCH 30	Lenten Feria | 17
MARCH 31	John Donne | 19

APRIL 1	Frederick Denison Maurice | 21
APRIL 2	Henry Budd | 24
APRIL 3	Richard, Bishop of Chichester | 27
APRIL 6	Monday in Holy Week | 30

April 7	Tuesday in Holy Week	33
April 8	Wednesday in Holy Week	36
April 9	Maundy Thursday	39
April 10	Good Friday	42
April 13	Monday in Easter Week	45
April 14	Tuesday in Easter Week	48
April 15	Wednesday in Easter Week	50
April 16	Thursday in Easter Week	53
April 20	Easter Feria	56
April 21	St. Anselm	60
April 22	Easter Feria	64
April 23	St. George, Martyr	67
April 24	Martyrs of the Twentieth Century	71
April 27	Easter Feria	75
April 28	Easter Feria	78
April 29	Catherine of Sienna	82
April 30	Marie de l'Incarnation	86

❦

May 1	St. Philip and St. James	90
May 4	Easter Feria	94
May 5	Easter Feria	98
May 6	St. John the Evangelist	102
May 7	Easter Feria	106
May 8	Julian of Norwich	110
May 11	Easter Feria	114

May 12	Florence Nightingale	118
May 13	Easter Feria	122
May 14	St. Matthias	126
May 15	Easter Feria	130
May 18	Rogation Day	134
May 19	Rogation Day	138
May 21	Ascension of the Lord	142
May 22	Easter Feria	146
May 25	Venerable Bede	150
May 26	Augustine of Canterbury	154
May 27	John Charles Roper	157
May 28	Easter Feria	161
May 29	Easter Feria	165
June 1	The Visit of the Blessed Virgin Mary to Elizabeth	169
June 2	Martyrs of Lyons: Blandina and Her Companions	173
June 3	The Martyrs of Uganda	177
June 8	Feria	181
June 9	Columba of Iona	185
June 10	Feria	189
June 11	Corpus Christi	193
June 15	Feria	197

Endnotes | 201

Introduction

On March 16, 2020, the Anglican Diocese of British Columbia ordered its parish churches to cease gatherings for worship and programming while we, along with the rest of the world, attempted to slow the course of the Covid-19 pandemic. Among the churches ordered to close was St. Barnabas, the parish of which I am the rector—a smallish, Anglo-Catholic parish near the edge of downtown Victoria.

A day or so after the order, I added to my morning prayers a simple written prayer. I wrote it without forethought, but after I'd done so, it seemed right to share that short prayer with the members of the congregation. So I sent it out by email as a sign from their rector that, even though we were unable to gather, even though we found ourselves physically separated, we were nevertheless held together in one body by the Holy Spirit. I had no thought, that day, of this becoming a daily practice. But the next day it felt right to do the same, and then also the day after that. It was only then that certain members of the parish realized—before I did!—that this was going to be a regular offering. I received after that third prayer a number of replies, thanking me and encouraging me in what I did not know I was setting off to do.

Søren Kierkegaard, the Danish philosopher and theologian, often used the metaphor of ocean swimming as a picture of how God moves us in faith: as we learn to pray, as we learn to give ourselves to him, God draws us out into ever deeper water. Slowly, through these prayers, God drew me out. The prayers grew longer and perhaps more searching as I tried, through them, to listen as intently as I could for God's word in me and in the unsettling circumstances we were finding ourselves in. Prayer is an exercise in the vulnerability of love. Although the fact that I knew I was going to share the prayer that was each morning's work and gift intensified the urgency of the discipline, yet as I wrote, only once or twice did the thought

Introduction

of having an audience impinge on the writing itself—and at these times only because I was addressing personal relations with individual people and had therefore to be circumspect in my wording.

As I continued to share—every weekday a new prayer—people in my parish began to inform me that they were incorporating them into their own daily prayers and sharing them in turn with family and friends, both locally and in places much further afield. A few urged me to publish them; and since this whole prayer ministry in an important sense took shape as a work of sharing with others, I hope that this request might also be fruitful in ways I cannot foresee. This is the reason I have seen these prayers (which some call "poems," but which were written as prayers) into print. I pray they will be helpful for others as well as those who first received them.

I dedicate this book to the people and parish of St Barnabas, Victoria, with whom the prayers were first shared, and as we strive to learn together, in faith, what it means to be the church. I am especially grateful to Bethany Murphy, Warden, who devoted many hours helping to prepare this manuscript for publication and whose dedication, loving wisdom, and enthusiasm is an encouragement to me and to us all.

Travis O'Brian

March 18
Cyril of Jerusalem

The Lord builds up Jerusalem;
    He gathers the outcasts of Israel.
He heals the brokenhearted,
    and binds up their wounds.

(Psalm 147:2–3)

Father of all,
we are in need of your comfort.
At this strange time, when many of us are sick
    or afraid of becoming
sick; when many of us are cut
    off from family, friends, colleagues,
the patterns that shape our daily life
    and shield us from anxiety and
    too much trouble;
when we are prevented from gathering
    as your church to worship
you, to receive your body and to be
made your body and so sent
    out to evidence the life which is
    your life: bless
us with the comfort of your Holy Spirit.

Free us from too much self-concern
    so that we may be
    a help and a support for others.
Help us, in all our actions, to remember
    your inexhaustible care
    for us and for the whole world.
Convert us, so that we rely only
on your hand waiting

        outstretched to steady and to hold us
and to catch us when we find
        ourselves falling
further into loneliness. Gird
        us in thanksgiving, for perfect
        love casts out every fear
in the name of our Savior, Jesus Christ.   Amen.

March 19
St. Joseph of Nazareth

I will sing of your steadfast love, O Lord, forever;
  with my mouth I will proclaim your faithfulness to all generations.

(Psalm 89:1–2)

Jesus Christ, Son of God,
today is Joseph's feast day,
  your earthly father:
Joseph, of whom we know so little that
we surmise he must have been
  a quiet man,
a man who listened more
  than he spoke, a man
who heard your Spirit's word in his soul and,
  even before you came to him,
understood what was required
  and was brave. Heavenly Father,
make us brave, make us
open-eared, waitful and brave
  like your servant Joseph was brave.

He was a good father.
He cared for the child you had given him
  to care for; he fed him, clothed him,
washed him; he taught him his trade and his faith.
He knew the pride of a father and
  the worries of a father.
And in all things he guided the child's increase
  in wisdom and stature.

Heavenly Father, make us like your servant Joseph,
  now especially, in this time of worry
and duress. Shape in us a heart

like his, a fatherly heart
> to care for Jesus as he did, through
our care for one another;
> a heart brave
in the name of your Son,
> who lived as one of us.   Amen.

March 20
Cuthbert, Bishop of Lindisfarne

The apostles gathered around Jesus, and told him all that they had done and taught. He said to them, "Come away to a deserted place all by yourselves and rest for a while."

(Mark 6:30–31)

Lord Jesus,
I sit here
at prayer in your empty church, wondering.
The doors are all locked.
The hymn books and the prayer
       books are stacked in cupboards;
the vestments removed and put into storage.
Sitting here, trying to listen into this disquieting
       silence, is to sense we are being
       emptied, poured out
like water, out
       of joint.

Until now, we have gathered, we have
       met together, every
       day, in this holy place
to worship: to sing psalms
       of thanksgiving, to call
on your presence, to express
       remorse, to be strengthened
by your body, to be renewed
       in our love for you, one
another, and your earth.

But today your church is empty.
The pews are like a wheat field after
       the harvest, waiting—for what?—

    in cold, quiet rows.
What, Lord, are you saying?
What are you asking of us?

Lord Jesus, you called
    your disciples into a desert place for rest.
Make this time of isolation to include
   also a gift of restoration.
Help us to use our solitude prayerfully, wisely, lovingly.
May it be a time of listening and
  growth for each of us,
renewal for your whole Body.
I cannot know, Lord, what
   you are preparing for us or
in us, but I pray
   that we may receive
   gifts we need but
for which we haven't known
   to ask.

May your people learn
   to take a step away
from the press of the world's
   expectations so that the whole
creation may take a breath and know
   that you are God.
It may be that we are to approach
this time of exile, of emptiness, as
   a kind of Holy Saturday:
learning how to wait
   for resurrection and new life. Amen.

MARCH 23
Gregory the Illuminator

The official said to him, "Sir, come down before my little boy dies." Jesus said to him, "Go; your son will live." The man believed the word that Jesus spoke to him, and started on his way.

(JOHN 4:49–50)

Father in Heaven,
yesterday, after hearing
      on the radio of the mounting
      death-tolls in Italy,
and that our government is now
      to restrict free border-crossings,
and that the residents of our islands
are shutting themselves away
      to protect themselves from others—
I felt a pang of panic for the first time,
disoriented, unsure
      suddenly of how I ought
      to feel or think or act;
unsure of what was right and wrong.
A quick pulse of fear overshadowed
      my instinct to care, to love, to share . . .

Lord, keep me from panic.
I know it is a sin.
It makes me deaf to your word,
      the hope by which I live.

Help me, my God,
to be like that official who only
had to hear Jesus say "your son will live,"
      to believe, trust, and return home—
though home was twenty infinitely long miles

   away. What were his thoughts
    during that eternal walk?
What doubts, panic, hope beyond hope,
   must have gripped his soul
in turns? Yet through all that upheaval,
   he believed.
He trusted. He kept walking.
And when at last he arrived,
he found not only his son restored to him
   but his own life restored as well.

O Lord, let thy mercy lighten upon us, as our trust is in thee.
O Lord, in thee have I trusted: let me never be confounded. Amen.

March 24

Lenten Feria

God is our refuge and our strength,
 a very present help in trouble.
Therefore we will not fear, though the earth should change,
 though the mountains shake in the heart of the sea . . .

 (Psalm 46:1–2)

Lord Jesus Christ,
days before he died,
your servant, Brother Lawrence,
 wrote from his heart:

> "The sorest afflictions are a burden only because of the way we look at them. . . .
> We must concentrate on knowing God: the more we know Him, the more we want to know Him. And the deeper and wider our knowledge, the greater will be our love. If our love of God is great, we shall love Him equally in sorrow and in joy."[1]

Lord, you know that I love you.
Yet all too often I am
overcome with worries, with
 frustrations, with a claustrophobic
hope for myself which makes me anxious
 about things I cannot change and hitches
me to that nagging pride which insists
 I need to prove myself
to you and others—as if
 I need to earn your love.
All these sins are cracks through which the joy of
 my faith leaks away.

Lord, you call us to be a people
      of joy. Restore me each day
to the joy of our faith, the joy of knowing
      we are loved. Especially now,
trapped in this time of uncertainty,
      lift our eyes up from the ground
that we might see your face and know you,
      and in knowing you, know ourselves
surrounded only by your tenacious
joy in Jesus Christ, our Lord.   Amen.

MARCH 25

The Annunciation of the Lord to the Blessed Virgin Mary

The Angel said to her, "Do not be afraid, Mary, for you have found favor with God. And now, you will conceive in your womb and bear a son, and you will name him Jesus. . . . For nothing will be impossible with God." Then Mary said, "Here am I, the servant of the Lord; let it be with me according to your word." Then the angel departed from her.

(LUKE 1:30–31; 37–38)

Father of all,
You are the life of the world.
You create us from nothing
     and sustain all things
        in the goodness of their being.
Do not forget us in our distress
     of unknowing.
Heal the sick and comfort the lonely.
Be yourself the peace of those who are anxious,
     the hope of those at a loss,
        the strength of those who are over-burdened,
the comfort of us all,
     your children.

Day by day and moment
     by moment,
help us to be more
     like Mary; to say "yes"
to the life that you give us
     to live, even when we find ourselves
in trouble; even when we find ourselves
     unable to understand.

Mary could not have known why

        the angel came to her
        that morning which was
so exactly like every other
        morning. She could not have known
why God broke in
        on her ordinary day, demanding,
asking of her
        things she could not have been,
        that moment, expected
to understand.

Mary did not know
        the aftermath
of her heart's "yes":
how her life would be
        charged with God,
        the mother of Jesus,
blessed with both the blessing
        and the sword.
Nevertheless, even so
unknowing, she poured
        her whole soul into her *yes*,
        her *let it be unto me*,
        her *here I am*.
Strange joy, to know one thing only:
that all would be well; that God had need of her;
that everything that needed to be done
        would be done.

Holy Father,
help us to be, like Mary,
        ready with our *yes*.
Fill us with her heart's
        joy and her body's
trust in your never-failing
        goodness, your never-failing
love for us and for all
        your children.   Amen.

March 26
Lenten Feria

The Father who sent me has himself testified on my behalf. You have never heard his voice or seen his form, and you do not have his word abiding in you, because you do not believe him whom he has sent. . . . You refuse to come to me to have life.

(John 5:37–38, 40)

Lord Jesus,
you are the word of life
both for those who love you
       and, I believe, even for those who refuse
you. You are the Father's
       pledge, to each and
to all, of his constant
love.

Lord Jesus, I believe that in you the fullness of love
       dwelt among us and remains
with us in the Spirit who shapes us in love's
way, the way in which you ordain
       us to live: creatures whose every
movement is to be a note in the song
       of great Thanksgiving.

But, Lord,
the scriptures set before us today are hard.
They tell of your anger
(when we made an idol, a golden calf,
       and fixed our hope on it instead of you);
and of your frustration
(when we shut our ears to the Father's word
       in your words, and rejected you).

Lord Jesus,
I do not believe that everything that pleases me
        is a sign of your pleasure.
Nor do I believe that everything that displeases me,
        or causes me to suffer,
        is a sign of your displeasure.
But I know that "real prayer is utterly truthful;
        and that this is what makes it hard."[2]
I want to know if you are angry with us now.
I want you to grant me faith enough to face that possibility,
not to dismiss it out of hand. I know,
because I am a parent, that
        anger can be one face of love.
Father, I want to know if you are angry with us.
Make me
        brave enough to face even the thought of it.

I want you to be truthful with us.
I want to hear what you are saying to us,
        what you need us to hear,
        even if I don't want to hear it.

You are our all in all: our beginning
        and our end; our hope and our life,
        and without you we can do nothing.
Help us, O Lord, always to give thanks to you,
        to trust that even if spoken in anger,
your word is love.

Help us, especially when it is hard,
        to hear and to know
        what you would have us do.   Amen.

March 27
Charles Henry Brent, Bishop

When the righteous call for help, the Lord hears,
    and rescues them from all their troubles.
The Lord is near to the brokenhearted,
    and saves the crushed in spirit.

(Psalm 34:17–18)

Spirit of God:
it is raining again today.
The clouds are low and heavy
    and I am feeling trapped, cooped up,
without even a small patch of blue sky to remind me
    of who I am.

I try to take a deep breath, to relax my shoulders,
to plant my feet firmly on the ground,
to sing—just loudly enough
    for you to hear me.

For a while my mind is too busy.
Prayer seems useless.
I am restless, but keep going
    from a sense of duty, or obligation, or something else.
At some point suddenly
    I seem to lose myself.
My soul turns
and begins to understand:
    it is not you
I am waiting for to hear me,
to join in on my prayer,
    but I am joining in on yours;
that these words I speak and sing are not my own,
    but they are your words speaking

        in me, through me;
that before I begin
        even to open my mouth, you
are there already,
        trying to catch my attention.

At some point my soul begins
        to understand that on a day
on which I am feeling lost,
        lost to you and to myself,
hoping without much hope that my prayer will find you,
        that I have it all backwards
and it is you who are seeking me.

        When the faithful call for help,
        the Lord hears

Spirit of God,
you hear our cry, for our crying out
for you is really your crying out
        for us;
and the love of those who seek you
is really your love
        seeking us;
and our hopes, our dreams of freedom,
        resurrection, fruition
of life, fullness of joy, feast-day of your unhesitating
        welcome, is our stirring
in the dawn of your promise—
if only we could begin
        to trust
that in every word of gratitude,
        in every longing for home,
        in every act of kindness or moment of patience,
        in every prayer, in every hymn of praise,
you are there already, calling us,
talking to us,
        waiting.   Amen.

March 30
Lenten Feria

Even though I walk through the valley of the shadow of death,
    I fear no evil;
for thou art with me;
    thy rod and thy staff, they comfort me.

                                          (Psalm 23:4, RSV)

Loving Father.
No one has ever seen you, but
is it too presumptuous to ask
    for just enough sight of you to know
for whom my heart reaches out when
    it reaches out for you;
just enough sight of you to know
why you mean so much to me
    and how it can possibly be
that I mean so much to you?

In loving you, is it for myself that I seek?
Yes, that must be it, in part—for I know this at least:
    that without you, I am nothing;
    that without you, everything I have done
    comes to nothing,
no matter how accomplished,
no matter how many people might know my name
    or admire my work.

But this cannot be the whole answer.
For I love you, Father, also in your Son—
who, yes, promises me rest, but who also
    demands me to be more than I am
or could ever even want to be, alone, without him.

He demands that I pick up my cross
        and follow him all the way to the end.

Holy Father, what will I find when I get there?
        You keep the answer to that question hidden in yourself.

You demand only that I love him with love enough
        to trust and to follow him,
even when he leads me to places
        it's hard to believe
you could want me to go;
to trust that when I follow him into those places,
follow him to the very end,
        you will be there, waiting for me,
to transform my love,
once and for all,
        into Joy.

Help me, Father,
help all of us to know how to take up and carry
        whatever cross you give us to carry.
Help us, Father,
to know how to love you even when
        love itself seems such a burden.
How can such a burden set us free?

Help us to know how to follow the footsteps of your Son.
We want so much to know the joy of being
        all you ask us to be, but
help us, Holy Father, in your mercy,
because we don't know how.   Amen.

March 31
John Donne

The fear of the Lord is clean, and endureth for ever;
  the judgements of the Lord are true, and righteous altogether.
More to be desired are they than gold, yea, than much fine gold;
  sweeter also than honey, and the honey-comb.

(Psalm 19:9–10, BCP)

Today, my God, I woke up tired,
my body unhappy and my mind unwilling
  to start the day.
When I sat down to pray, I couldn't focus.
Even the grey light sifting reluctantly through the window
  seemed to drain me.

Sometimes on days like today you reward me,
and even when I expect nothing, you lead me out
  into places of wonder.
You draw me closest to you, sometimes, when I least expect it;
and I am filled, at those moments, with such gratitude
along with a feeling like peace
  which carries me through the day.

I half-hoped today might be like that.
All I have to do, I thought, is begin.
And so I did. But the words ran
  through me like water through fingers.
Nothing caught, nothing held.
Today, if you led me out at all, it was only
  past houses I can see from my window and am tired of looking at,
  places which seem to me can have nothing new to say.

And yet I am also, somehow, strangely comforted.
Even bored with myself

    and bored with my prayer,
another part of me is certain
    that this day too is something I must need,
that nothing is for nothing because you are always at work in me,
    purifying me, transforming me, even when I am too numb
    to be aware.

So somehow, even today, a diffused
   ray slips through:
not quite a cure for this
fatigue, but I concede the greyness
   too tests who I must be,
and that this sullenness of soul's
   both a trial of my self-insistence and
   your mark on my back: the trace
of a word declaring
   I must turn,
turn and wait
   for the daylight
to rise
in me and overwhelm in golden thankfulness
   my thankless soul.

from Good Friday, 1613. Riding Westward (John Donne)

   Let mans Soule be a Spheare, and then, in this,
   The intelligence that moves, devotion is,
   And as the other Spheares, by being growne
   Subject to forraigne motion, lose their owne,
   And being by others hurried every day,
   Scarce in a yeare their naturall forme obey:
   Pleasure or businesse, so, our Soules admit
   For their first mover, and are whirld by it.
   Hence is't, that I am carryed towards the West
   This day, when my Soules forme bends toward the East.
   There I should see a Sunne, by rising set,
   And by that setting endlesse day beget . . . Amen.

April 1
Frederick Denison Maurice

"Lord, when was it that we saw you hungry and gave you food, or thirsty and gave you something to drink?"... And the king will answer them, "Truly I tell you, just as you did it to one of the least of these who are members of my family, you did it to me."

(Matthew 25:37, 40)

Father of all,
the house is very quiet.
It is early still, and the family is asleep.

I am grateful to you for the quiet.
It is precious time, time you give
      for me to be alone with myself and with you,
time in which to search the map of my life.

And yet, Father,
however grateful I am for the time you give me to be alone,
      I am even more grateful for the gift of my family,
whose love, I have needed to learn,
      makes it possible for me to *be* alone,
      possible for the loneliness to be different than just loneliness,
      and for these moments of quiet to be free
and full of more than just myself.

Thank you, Father, for each of my children,
      whose lives, so precious to you, you have placed in my care
      and in whom you have blessed my life
in ways I once could never have dreamed that I wanted but
      (I have needed to learn),
I really do want and need—perhaps even more,
     in a different way, than they need me.

Thank you, Father, for Jasmin,
who you have given me to share all that I have
        and all that I am—
on whom I secretly depend for this quietness of heart,
        and so also, in a mysterious way, for my prayer,
which is both hers and mine.

Father, bless my family.
These days we are more together than we are used to being.
Sometimes tempers flare.
Often I find there is just too much noise,
        too many bodies in a small space,
        too many demands.
But there are also unexpected gifts:
        the children enjoying each other,
teaching one another, needing each other.

Bless us and show us how, by giving us
        to belong to one another, you are bringing us
to know what we most need to learn:
        what love is, and so how dearly
we belong to you.

Father,
watch over all who are alone, isolated in their houses—
especially the elderly and those who have no family
        or whose families are far away.
Give them to know
        how dearly they belong to you,
        and so, although they are alone,
they are never alone.

Father,
bless our St. Barnabas family.
You have given us also to belong to one another,
        in order to teach us how to be your people,
        in order for us to learn what love is

and so how to live together as an example of the life
    you are preparing in us.

Help us, Holy Father.
We are your children.
There is not one who is outside
    your family.
Help us to serve you by sharing
    the one life
of your whole household.
In the name of your Son.   Amen.

April 2
Henry Budd

Let the hearts of those who seek the Lord rejoice.
Seek the Lord and his strength;
    seek his presence continually.

(Psalm 105:3–4)

Holy God,
I have so very little to complain about.
My family is healthy; we still have work;
and unlike friends in Italy and New York,
we have space in our house to move
    and, when we need,
        to get out of one another's way.
The beach is close by, and we are still able to walk out
and enjoy the sunshine, glad in the signs
    of spring coming on.
There is even a hummingbird's nest in the butterfly bush
in our backyard, the two fledgling hummingbirds
    keeping their mother busy
    and delighting us all.
Though they are small and delicate,
the life-energy in them, their hunger
    for the food of life, is so strong.
They are hungry all the time,
    restless to grow
    out of their tiny nest and fly.

Father,
I have so little to complain about.
Forgive me my own restlessness,
    but I am also hungry—for food I must wait for you
    to provide.
I am also restless for wings, restless to grow

into the fullness of the life you hold out for us,
restless to grow into the being I believe
      you have destined me to be.
"Destined" sounds a bit grandiose—and maybe
it is only the sin of pride speaking, or anxiety.
On the other hand, maybe it's through my restlessness
      that you turn my face upward,
waiting and hungry to be filled entirely
      with you—with your Spirit,
      the life of my life.

Lord, I am painfully aware
      that I have no right to complain about anything.
Forgive me. I know I am impatient.
I know I should be satisfied
      with all I have been given.
But I am not satisfied. I am constantly afraid
      that the life I am leading is
      not all I am meant for,
that there is something more you need from me.
      Only, I don't know what.

Forgive me, Lord. I know I ought to be satisfied
      with your grace alone.
I know your grace is everything,
      but I am even afraid of being satisfied.
I am afraid peace would mean settling for too little,
      almost too mean a life.

More than just "satisfaction," I want—but I don't really know
      what it is that I want. I want
to be over-full. Not with material things:
      it is enough just to be satisfied with them.
I mean over-full with the life that makes our heart flood
      with delight in the springtime, with Easter joy.

Father, forgive my impatience.
I know there can be no spring
        without winter; no Easter without the cross.
I always want to be ahead of myself.
I want to live, but am troubled by death.
I want to love cleanly and purely, but
        I'm troubled by all this hunger in me.

Feed me, heavenly Father,
with wisdom to know myself
        a creature of your own heart and hand.
Give me the patience you require
        to die
trusting the one thing needful:
that, however small the circumstance in which
        we find you place us,
however restricted our energies,
        influence, our opportunities
for action; however insignificant
        our life may seem compared to the enormous
promise you place like a seed
        within us,
in you we fill the universe
        and are free.   Amen.

April 3
Richard, Bishop of Chichester

The Jews took up stones again to stone him. Jesus replied, "I have shown you many good works from the Father. For which of these are you going to stone me?" The Jews answered, "It is not for a good work that we are going to stone you, but for blasphemy, because you, though only a human being, are making yourself God."

(John 10:31–33)

Father of our Lord Jesus,
we are drawing quickly towards Holy Week,
    a week which demands
we turn to face ourselves and be
    terrifyingly honest
about ourselves in our relationship
    to your Son.
Holy Week is always, for me, a sea of clashing,
    unruly emotions, as we follow Jesus
into the holy city and are swept
    up in the palms and praise of the people;
as we climb behind him up the stone
    stairs into the upper room
    to be shown there what service is
and ardent humility, suffering him
    to wash
our (to us) unlovely feet;
to taste there what faithfulness is
    in the gift
of himself in the meal of bread and wine;
as we observe the circle of persecution tighten to a noose,
    and as we flee;
as we climb behind him to the place
    of the skull

where there is nothing we can do
        but weep and watch him die;
as we approach his tomb in the dim light
        to learn there what forgiveness is:
the lengths to which you go and to which
      you are going to restore us
          to life.

Father of our Lord Jesus,
Holy Week is almost here.
And the scriptures daily describe how Jesus's enemies
        are closing in.

It is easy, when reading, to think of his enemies
        as our enemies,
for they are after the blood of one we love
        and we know how it will end.
But, Holy Father, I am not at all sure,
in fact I am most uncomfortably uncertain
that, if I were there, I would not be among them—
        his persecutors:
not because I am a vigilante for the status quo,
        a too-rigid enforcer of tradition or law;
not because I am particularly ignorant, unobservant,
        or hard of heart,
but just because I love you—and it hurts me
        to see you dishonoured. It angers me
when people attempt to squeeze you
        into boxes much too finite
        and all too human.

Holy Father,
generation after generation, your people
        waited and prepared for the coming of your Christ.
And when, after all those hundreds of years,
        he came at last among them,
they did not recognize him.
They persecuted him and killed him.

They killed him because they loved you,
> because they wanted to protect, to keep sacred,
> the holiness of your name.
The one you sent as the servant of all
> they killed, believing
> they were serving you.

Holy God,
Jesus scathingly called *hypocrites*
those who can read the signs of coming weather,
> but cannot read the signs of his coming.
Is it possible that even my love for you
> creates blind spots in my soul?

Lord Jesus,
you know that I love you,
> and I believe you are the son of the living God.
But who do we tend to persecute,
> to grieve, the most but those
we love most? Lord Jesus,
I want to know you when you come,
> though I am certain it will happen
in a way I cannot now imagine or expect.
I want to be among
> those who recognize you
because they must be the ones
> who have already met you;
because their lives are
> the glass from which your face
looks out.

Lord Jesus, help us
> to follow you faithfully this Holy Week.
Open the eyes of our hearts to see
> the signs of your coming.   Amen.

April 6

Monday in Holy Week

How precious is your steadfast love, O God!
  All people may take refuge in the shadow of your wings....
For with you is the fountain of life;
  in your light we see light.

(Psalm 36:7, 9)

Holy Father,
here we are in Holy Week.
Jesus has already entered the city,
  welcomed with yesterday's palms and Hosannas.
Mary, led, perhaps, by her love's wisdom
  more than her understanding,
has already anointed you, with her tears and hair,
  for burial.
All the pieces are set.
Minute by minute, the hour approaches.
  And Jesus's own heart,
  bared in every word,
wrings out the prayer
  not mine, but your will,
  your will be done.

Holy Father,
every day during this time of isolation and exile,
  during this time we have been unable to gather in your name,
  unable to make our Eucharist,
every day I also pray
Your will be done.

But Father,
as the days begin to blur together,
to jostle up against each other

        like anonymous commuters on a moving train;
as we draw towards the heart of Holy Week,
it gets more difficult to understand
        what this exile is really for.
What really is it, if anything,
        that you are preparing in us?

Although next to all that your Son
        must this week suffer: the pain of the cross
        he knows will tear his body,
the pain of abandonment
        he knows will tear his soul;
although next to the whole scope of the world's suffering,
this exile is such a little thing,
        it does not seem a little thing to me.

This is, no doubt, much too self-concerned.
But Holy Week, in so many ways,
        is the pin around which the wheel of our year turns;
itself so clear and distinct,
        holding the whirring outer edges in.

This week you always work so hard in me,
        drawing me out in so many ways,
        my heart and my mind,
challenging me to acknowledge the shadows
        —exhausting me, keeping me up night and day.
This week you always work so hard
        to open the blind spots of my eyes,
        to open the locked places of my heart.
You lead me from having to hear my own voice in the crowd
    yell "Crucify!"
        right up to the foot of the cross
where the blood in my veins stirs
with the blood of your head, hands, side—
    my God!
which somehow gives me strength
to look up and to bow down,

   to kiss your mangled feet
in a confusion of adoration and pity: self-pity
stirred up with such helpless pity for you—
  my God!
which somehow gives me the strength to go
from the cross into that strange
    house of waiting, Holy Saturday . . .
a day which, to my surprise, though I'm sure
   is meant as a day of mourning,
never fails, rain or shine,
    to embody the whole season of spring.
Stirred by something we cannot see,
it is a day of preparation for something
   we cannot imagine, something being readied
underground, deep in the recesses of the earth . . .
until the universe narrows to a voice:
   Woman, why are you weeping?
   Whom do you seek?
and bursts into flower with shouts of Hallelujah!
Hallelujah!

Holy Father,
why must we be kept now
from making this journey with you
   with each other?
Why are you holding us off,
keeping us at a distance?
I feel today a little like Mary must have felt
   when she washed her Lord's feet with her tears.
I don't understand this parting.
But I trust, through everything, you are teaching me
   to pray and to desire
Your will be done. Amen.

April 7

Tuesday in Holy Week

Walk while you have the light, so that the darkness may not overtake you. . . .
While you have the light, believe in the light, so that you may become children
of light.

(John 12:35, 36)

Holy Jesus,
I try to imagine what this week
      must have been like for you.
All those people in the bustling city, the streets
      crowded with vendors and pilgrims,
clamoring for your attention, constantly asking you questions—
      some, in their heart's yearning, to learn from you,
      some to gossip later with their neighbors,
      some to catch you out to destroy you.

All of that noise and dust and duplicity
when your whole desire was only to give
      the bread each one needed to live.

It must have been exhausting,
      having to be so constantly vigilant,
      having to examine every heart,
      having to listen, not so much to the words directed at you,
but for the spirit—
whether a question grew from a broken, sincere heart,
      or sowed seeds of malice.

Now is the judgment of the world,
      you told them—the judgment they themselves brought
down by the spirit in which they approached you,
      questioned you, took up your words.

Holy Jesus,
it must have been exhausting,
        having to weigh every question,
whether it peered from dark doorways
        or sought the streets of light.
It must have been exhausting
to give to each an answer: a word
        to confound the darkness; a word
        to encourage the light.

Holy Jesus,
when I imagine you under this strain,
I can understand why you needed
        to escape the crowd, why
        "you departed and hid."
But please, Holy Jesus,
do not depart from me.
Do not hide from me.

Sitting here, in the twilight of this morning,
        looking to quieten my heart in prayer,
I also desire to come to you,
to ask you to be near me, to hear me, to answer me,
        even when I'm not even sure
        what I mean when I pray,
what I am asking for—or what I need
        to ask for.

Though I know only too well that I am
        a weed-bed of questions,
today, thinking of your strain,
        I am emptied of questions.
Though I know only too well that I am
        a tangled nest of needs,
today, thinking of your suffering,
        I am emptied of need.
Today, knowing, as you knew, all that is coming,

    I don't know what to hope for.

I don't know anything, Holy Jesus,
        except that I want you show yourself to me,
        except that I want you
            to permit me, too, to address you;
that you might examine my heart also.

You alone can read what's there.

This morning, I pray that you find,
        rising up from under all the confusion,
        this one prayer:
Holy Jesus, though I fear the darkness,
        make me a child of your light.   Amen.

April 8

Wednesday in Holy Week

Who will contend with me?
*   Let us stand up together.*
Who are my adversaries?
*   Let them confront me.*
It is the Lord God who helps me;
*   who will declare me guilty?*

(Isaiah 50:8–9)

Holy Jesus,
today is Wednesday, tomorrow Thursday,
        the next day, Friday.
These are the days of growing shadow,
days of darkness pushing
        from the outer edges of the world,
        from the hidden edges of our lives,
in toward the center.

Lord Jesus,
today we read that you are troubled in spirit,
aware as you are of the coming darkness,
aware as you are that one who calls you "Lord"
        and whom you call *friend*
will betray you.

It is true, Lord,
that I find a shadow on the edges of my heart also,
        for I know, of course, or think I know,
what the next days will bring; and I am confused—
        burdened and confused—
by the part I will play in them: by my betrayal
and denial, by my ignorance and self-seeking
        and wanting always to go my own way;

even by my presumptions of holiness,
        all the ways I am one of the crowd,
the market square crammed with people, yelling
    Crucify!

Lord,
I am aware of the shadow on the edges of my heart,
       just thinking about the days ahead.
But I find something else there too.
Today I find that I am walking more with your disciples
     than I am with you.
Although they must feel that somewhere something has shifted;
that you are growing introspective and solemn;
       that opinions and chatter and accusations
are swirling around in the city.
At the same time, it seems they cannot help
but be confident and even happy in their faith
      that you are in control,
         that you understand what they cannot,
        that you have a plan,
         that God is with you and thus with them.
I am sure, as they overhear the whispers in the streets,
feel fingers pointing behind their backs,
      that they are even a little bit proud,
for they are your disciples and chosen friends who believe
    if God is for us, who can be against us?

Today, Lord, I realize that I am with the disciples,
     a little wary of the day
but happy to be busy readying for the Passover
and preparing for the meal you have directed them to prepare;
happy making lists, arranging the sharing of responsibilities,
       purchasing food, setting the table,
finding joy in all these familial and familiar things—
familiarities which sustain us and which too are a kind of prayer,
deflecting our worries as they do about what tomorrow
      or the day after
might bring.

Holy Lord,
today my spirit is more with the disciples than with you.
For today the disciples are busy.
Today they are sure only that the Passover is approaching,
        and that this year is unusual and particularly special
since this year they will celebrate
        with you.

Holy Jesus,
I pray that being with your disciples is enough,
        at least for today.
Today the light is still with us a little longer;
today I feel the earth warming in the spring sunshine,
        the sky so unselfconsciously blue;
and the joy of this world, and the life stirring in it,
and happiness in the work you have given us to do.
I pray, Lord, that you will accept this unexpected gift
        as my offering to you, for today;
that you do not count it as forgetfulness—
        either of you or of myself;
and you will not count it against me
        as untoward pride that, when I hear you ask
Who will contend with me?
Let us stand up together
        I want to count myself among those
        standing up with you.   Amen.

April 9

Maundy Thursday

I called on the name of the Lord:
   "O Lord, I pray, save my life!"
Gracious is the Lord, and righteous;
   our God is merciful.

(Psalm 116:4–5)

Heavenly Father,
your Spirit is the Life of all life,
and by your Word you restore all lost things to yourself.
As I look toward the gifts and challenges
   tonight will bring—the thanksgiving
   and misgiving, the wonder, the silence,
the fatigue—I am at a loss.
The grace of this night, the whole long journey of this night,
is food for the body, is food and drink for the whole body,
   and not for each one alone, as if a hand could live
      without its arm, or an arm
      without its shoulder, the shoulder
      without its neck, head, heart, lungs.
The spirit of this night is life for the one body
whose duty and purpose and joy is to be
      the Priesthood of the great thanksgiving,
      the Prophet of the wonder,
      the Mid-wife of your love
in the world you have given us to serve.

But, Heavenly Father,
how can we be what you have called us to be,
   how can we receive this grace, live your life,
      be braced by your Spirit in the way
   as hands without arms,
arms without shoulders—alone, separated

  from the wholeness of your holy body?

Tonight, by the example of your Son,
who, by washing his disciples' feet, upended
  the hierarchies of servitude,
you showed us a new way of living, a way in which
  power is not power,
  in which glory is not glory,
  in which service is perfect freedom.
But, Heavenly Father,
how are we to live your new commandment,
  how are we
to wash one another's feet
  when the church is empty,
when there is no one's feet to wash?

Tonight we remember
that it was on this day your Son was betrayed—and yet,
at supper with his friends,
  he took bread and blessed it,
  took wine and gave you thanks,
promising all—from that day to the end of days—
  who in his name would gather, he would be
with them
  among them
  in them,
feeding us wholly with the life
  of his whole body.

Holy God,
in the gift of the Eucharist you gave us to be
  the priesthood of thanksgiving
for all of your creation.
You called us to witness the Lord's death
  and resurrection in the joy of our body,
  our one Easter body.
But how are we to be
  the body of thanksgiving,

>   to celebrate Holy Communion,
> torn as we are from communion
>   with those with whom you have given us
> to be your people,
> your church?
>
> Tonight we remember how,
> at the hour of crisis,
>   we fall asleep;
> how, when your hour comes,
>   we deny knowing you,
>   how we flee from your side
>   and scatter into darknesses, afraid.
>
> Tonight, Lord Jesus,
> we remember your broken body,
>   poured out like water, the bones
> torn joint from joint—hand from its arm,
>   arm from its shoulder.
>
> Help us tonight, Father.
> Heal us. Repair your broken body.
>
> Help us to be wakeful, watchful, trustful
>   that even when we have no eyes to imagine
>   how healing will come,
> that it will come.
> And that even when we are no longer
>   able to dream of how we might be restored
> that restoration will come:
>   and we will be
> returned to you, to one another,
>   to the life and work you have given us,
>   to the body of glory
> you are consecrating us to be.   Amen.

April 10

Good Friday

All we like sheep have gone astray;
we have turned every one to his own way;
and the Lord has laid on him
the iniquity of us all.

(Isaiah 53:6 RSV)

Lord Jesus,
how has it come to this?

There was a day in my life,
a yet-unfinished day,
when I began
to waken to a voice I had heard
everyday but had never heard
until then. It was your voice,
inviting me, demanding me, inviting me
to look for the thing I needed most to find,
     my self,
in you.

Lord Jesus,
wherever did it happen, that I lost the thread
     of my own life?
How is it possible to have gotten separated
     from what is closest to me?

Each morning when I get up,
     the wind in the tree tells me
    see, all is vanity.
Each night when I lay down again,
the water in the creek tells me

> *there is nothing here but hunger:*
> *even the sea is never full.*

Lord Jesus,
you have told me where to find
all that I need to be all
that I am.

Lord Jesus,
you have told me I need only seek for you,
follow you;
that in your life I find my own.

Why, then,
do I look in a thousand different directions,
the eyes of my mind and of my heart
      restless, curious, unsettled, wanting
everything—looking everywhere and
anywhere, in fact, just to avoid looking at
      your looking at me.

Lord Jesus,
why do I do this? Do I only pretend
      to want what I most want?
Why do I hang back,
distract myself with this and that,
fantasize about all the things I need
when all I need is to turn my face: *here I am.*
      Here I am.

Lord Jesus,
You have said, "Follow me."
But—there you are, hanging,
thirsty and dying, on a cross.
How has it come to this?
Who put you there?

Lord Jesus,

Why do I call out to you only ever as a last resort?
Why is it only when I have nothing *left* to give
      that I give myself to you?

Lord Jesus,
is it because I am afraid that to come to you
means having to go the whole way,
      the whole way you have gone for me?
Is it to *that* place you demand I follow?
But—there you are, standing
right beside me, walking
right beside me.
And it is your voice I hear
      quietly speaking my name.

Why then does it feel such a distance
      that I must cross?
I don't know how to cross it.
I don't know.
What are you asking of me?

Instead of stopping to wait for you,
instead of waiting and listening,
instead of trusting you to cross every distance—
      the distance separating me from you;
      the distance separating me from myself;
      the distance separating the necessity of death
          from the promise of life—
I scatter myself like a dandelion, little seeds
      blowing in all directions.

Lord Jesus,
I want so much to live.
Why are you hanging there, dying,
on a cross?
Who put you there?
How has it come to this
      between you and me?

April 13

Monday in Easter Week

So they left the tomb quickly with fear and great joy and ran to tell his disciples. Suddenly, Jesus met them and said, "Greetings!" And they came to him, took hold of his feet, and worshiped him.

(Matthew 28:8–9)

Lord Jesus,
when I pray to you,
    when I lift up my eyes
    and my voice and my heart
in thanksgiving and wonder;
when I say to you, "Blessed are you, Lord,
    you came from God; you are my salvation,"
I don't know exactly what I *mean*
    by that word.
I only know that no other word
comes anywhere close to all I want
    or all I need
    to say.

There are, no doubt, a thousand things
from which I need saving—sins
    and fears and hypocrisies and pretensions,
      my too-easy conformities to this world
      and the comforts of privilege—
but when your Easter word
Greetings; do not be afraid
drops into that chamber reserved for it
    in my heart,
I'm not thinking about these things.
Perhaps I ought to be, but I'm not.

It is hard to describe how I feel,

        when you greet me:
something like the blueness of the blue sky;
something like the young hummingbirds must feel
        the moment they discover what their wings are for;
something like morning light
        filtering through the forest trees.

All I know is that you have come looking also for me;
        with *my* name also on your heart—
you who makes sense of my senselessness,
        who blesses my life,
        who is the hope of all my actions.
You have come to me—how and from where
        I don't really know, but
you have come looking for me
        with a promise my soul receives
        with quick *joy*—
            reaching out for it,
knowing it like a thirsting animal
        knows water.

Here you are, my Lord, greeting me with the promise
        that nothing in my life which is good,
nothing in it which contains light enough
        in which to see your own reflection,
will be lost
        or darkened forever:
but will be and is kept in God,
treasured and precious to him,
        delightful to him;
        very good: an apple tree
among all the trees of the wood.

Lord Jesus.
You are what God delights in
        when he delights in me.
You are my light and my love,
        my beginning, my end,

my salvation, my Hallelujah!

Today, at least, I am full of light
        and I am
            not afraid.   Amen.

April 14

Tuesday in Easter Week

Rejoice in the Lord. . . .
    Praise the Lord with the lyre. . . .
The earth is full of the steadfast love of the Lord.

(Psalm 33:1, 2, 5)

Lord Jesus Christ,
we hear and see and know
    your promise of joy everywhere,
if only we take the time to praise you
    and learn to know you through our prayers.

This morning there has been an indefatigable robin
singing his heart out in the chestnut tree
    for nearly an hour now.
I once read an ornithologist state
    that birds never sing for joy.
I don't think that ornithologist
could have been a man of prayer.
Is it possible to spread joy
  without knowing joy?

My robin of course does not know the word "joy";
    and no doubt his call is so urgent
    because the spring weather
      insists that it's time for him to seek a mate.
But how could his song
    call up such joy in me—if it were not already
    joyful?

When I open the window to listen,
  I also hear, under his strong tenor,
the sweet sonatina of a finch,

then a mischievous wren, a towhee,
        and some other bird I cannot name.
Lord, I take such delight in them.
Their songs fill my heart as if
        they hold the secret
        of the purest form of prayer.

I don't know why their songs affect me as they do.
But I feel it must be *their* job to lift up my heart
        and then *my* job to insert into their song
        your name
so that together our praise
        may be more complete.

I feel it must be their job to provide the key
        in which your name ought to be sung:
        as spontaneous and pure as instinct.

The robin helps me to believe,
Lord, that nothing we do
        we do alone;
and that nothing we say,
not even our most intimate words,
        we say alone.

For you, Lord, are the Joy
marrying the robin's song and my prayer
        into a single offering of joy.
You are the Beauty
marrying the morning light and the light in me
        into one leap of praise.
You are the Life
uniting all your creatures
        in the one great work of thanksgiving.
You are the Love
uniting everything that is in you who is
        our all in all. Hallelujah!   Amen.

April 15

Wednesday in Easter Week

And he said to them, "What were you discussing with each other while you walk along?" They stood still, looking sad. Then one of them, whose name was Cleopas, answered him, "Are you the only stranger in Jerusalem who does not know the things that have taken place there in these days?"

(Luke 24:17–18)

Lord Jesus,
there's certainly lots of discussion in these days,
lots of talking as we walk the lengthening road
      of this shutdown.
There is indeed lots of opinion, speculation, worry.
There are indeed many who are sad, stressed,
      feeling claustrophobic,
          as if the walls of their lives are falling
in on them.

Although the authorities feed us daily
      a diet of numbers and warnings and strategy,
when I listen to them, I cannot hear
the one word I'm so anxious to hear:
      that I will be safe,
      that the people I love will be safe,
      that the church will be safe,
      that all my plans and my hopes
will be safe.

Lord, in the face of so much uncertainty,
      it's hard to keep silent.
I find myself, almost against my will,
adding my voice to all the talk—
      the projecting of infection rates,

        the comparing of exit strategies.
Lord, in the face of so much uncertainty,
it's hard just to wait,
        to wait without knowing;
and I find myself, almost against my will,
adding my voice to the talk—
unconsciously hoping, perhaps,
that talking must be a kind of knowing,
        providing, for the moment,
        a kind of comfort.

But when I remove myself,
when I listen in on the noisy round of opinions
(and I too have opinions!)
what I hear is not really speech,
        not really words,
but the crying voices of your people—
even those who do not know you enough
to call upon your name:
        We are vulnerable, Lord, and anxious.
        We don't know how all this will end.
        We don't know how all we love will be taken care of.
        We don't know what to do.

Lord Jesus,
when I am in need of comfort to sustain me,
the talking and talking only makes me more anxious.
When I am in need of comfort,
I find it in silence,
in the prayer by which you quieten
        my over-busy soul, quieten
        the over-busy world in me enough
for your word to come near me
        on the road.

This morning, I have been trying, Lord,
        in silence
to see our empty church

      as an image of your empty tomb.
I have been trying to see it,
not as a sign of sadness, disappointed hope,
      or even death,
but as a sign that you are preparing something,
      something for which we can only wait and watch
      before we can understand.

This morning, Lord, I have been trying to see
your empty church as the sign of *new life coming*;
I have been trying to understand how
      our inability to understand
is a lesson that you are teaching us—
      a lesson in patience
      and in knowing how to wait;
      a lesson in reverence,
      and in knowing how to listen rather than talk;
      a lesson in how to be vulnerable,
      in how to receive rather than give;
      a lesson in how to live in grace;
      a lesson in how to be loved.

In all times of tribulation;
in all times of prosperity;
in the hour of death and in the day of judgement,
good Lord, deliver us.   Amen.

April 16

Thursday in Easter Week

While in their joy they were disbelieving and still wondering, [Jesus] said to them, "Have you anything here to eat?" They gave him a piece of broiled fish, and he took it and ate it in their presence.

(Luke 24:41–43)

Lord Jesus,
it is hard right now
to plan anything,
    and having to do so,
        trying to see too far ahead,
makes me anxious and nervous.

Whenever people ask me about our plans;
when I hear people say, "We are in this for the long haul,"
    and hear the already-haggard tone of their voices,
    and observe the stress etched already in their faces;
when I begin to worry about our church,
    our beautiful community,
    our people, our finances—
even now, just addressing these concerns to you,
    my vulnerability and the tension,
you make me aware
    of how much I live in the future,
    of how much
worry for what I cannot change
takes away from the abundance
    and the beauty
of my life. For here I am,
mind and heart unsettled; uncertain, worried,
    while just outside my window the day
is beautiful and holds already so much
more—the gold-green of the new leaves singing in the early sun—

than I could ever know to ask for or imagine.

Perhaps this is the lesson you have for me this hour:
        how much of my life I spend
waiting for my life—gazing across the water,
        wondering when the horizon
        will begin to move toward me:
my habit of acting as if my life will begin
        later—
as if the present, what I'm doing now,
        is not the real thing, but a preparation, a prelude
for the moment my life will begin in earnest;
for the moment when the picture
        I've so long nourished, of a life in which my love
will daily flourish and in which I will be happy and free—
will come, and I will begin to be
        the man I have believed I am
given, asked, called, driven
        to be.

Lord Jesus, on the day of your resurrection
you came among your disciples and said to them,
        "Peace be with you."
Then you ate with them a piece of broiled fish—
as if to demonstrate that no moment had greater reality
        than that moment;
as if to show them that the life they had been dreaming of
        was right there with them,
        that they had only to open their hands
and their eyes, their mouths
        and their hearts: and it would be
there, with them, in them,
        fullness of life!

Lord Jesus, my mind is unsettled today.
But I believe I understand:
where you are, that is where
        my life is,

and you are right here, now,
        with me, in this prayer.
I believe I understand:
you alone, O Lord, are my future,
        and so all that I am and all that I have to be
        is, therefore, this moment, here.

Help me, Lord,
        to live, today, in the assurance of your presence.
Help me not to be anxious
        about what I cannot change.
Help me to trust in your love for me
     and to know that just to know
you are standing closer to me
        than I am to myself
is all I need to know, today,
        and for the future.
Help me, Lord. For in you is life, my life.
You are my happiness.
In you alone I am free.   Amen.

April 20
Easter Feria

Do not be astonished that I said to you, "You must be born from above." The wind blows where it chooses, and you hear the sound of it, but you do not know where it comes from or where it goes. So it is with everyone who is born of the Spirit.

(John 3:7–8)

Holy Father,
the earth bears on its body
the marks of your love,
and everything that is
      reflects in its own being
the light of your being,
        shining out of the darkness.

On those days in which I feel most alive,
      awake, and full of the energy of wonder,
on those days and moments
      when I almost touch, it feels to me,
      that original delight with which
      you speak the word of life,
I feel so complete, filled up,
as if there could not possibly be anything
      left to ask for, anything more
I could possibly need.

Holy Father,
I try to store up those moments
      as precious gifts
so that on normal days—days such as today—
days when there seems to be a thin film
      of "everydayness" between the earth and the sun,

I can bring them out to remind me
        of your word's stamp on me;
that although one day seems so often just to smear wearily into the next,
        the gift you have given me,
        the gift of myself,
you intend for something.
The day is not to be used up
        bleary-eyed or pining for what is not,
but in the practice of loving;
        wakefulness to what is.

Holy Father,
every day I pray, "Thy will be done."
And although I pray those words sincerely,
        I admit that part of me is afraid of them,
for I don't know what it is that I am praying for.

Those words demand a frightening abyss of trust.
They demand we give over our own
        ideas, visions, hopes for ourselves
and hopes for the world—even the ones
        we believe are faithful, "Christian," and good.
So although I believe, and although I trust you
        when I pray to you, secretly
I don't trust that I trust.

For you know that I haven't even learned
        to trust and accept each day as it comes,
asking of it nothing for myself,
asking of it only your will for me,
        how I am to serve you in it;
        how I am to be nothing
but a reflection of your light.
Instead, I approach each day
        as if it should serve *me*,
as if the day should feed *me*
        with the life that I crave.

I pray, "Give us this day our daily bread."
You yourself have put these words
        into my mouth,
but I am unsure, again, what it is
        that I am asking for.
Is it for the food I want or think that I need
        if I am to be the person I want
        to believe I am?

Or is this prayer for daily bread
        your way of reminding me
that the only true hunger
    is for the food with which
        you have already fed me—
that I am to trust completely, therefore,
        in your provision?

Or, Holy Father,
        do you leave me hungry on purpose—
otherwise, how could I hunger and thirst
        for you?

Loving Father,
help me to know the difference
between my self-will
        and your will working
        through me and for me.
Help me to know the difference
between appetites that pull me away from you
    and appetites that draw me closer—
        appetites which are *themselves* food
because your Spirit fills us even in our longing
        for your Spirit.

Loving Father,
bring me into the fullness of this day.
Feed me with your presence,

   waken me to your will,
and teach me, today,
       how I am
to live by the light of your Son.   Amen.

April 21
St. Anselm

There was a Levite, a native of Cyprus, Joseph, to whom the apostles gave the name Barnabas (which means "son of encouragement"). He sold a field that belonged to him, then brought the money, and laid it at the apostles' feet.

(Acts 4:36–37)

Lord our God,
you are the Father of all things
and in you the whole of creation
       is one family.
Your child Francis taught us to understand ourselves
in this beautiful way,
       preaching to the birds,
       calling "brother" the sun, wind, and fire,
    calling "sister" the moon, water, earth,
         and even death—which you tamed on the Cross
and brought into your household.

Holy Father,
we talk often about the "human family."
We speak too of the one holy catholic church
       as a family in Christ Jesus, your Son.
And I like to look upon our parish church,
the people of St. Barnabas,
       as a family—
a family of individuals you have given to each other
       so that we might learn
         to serve and love you *in* each other;
so that we might learn what it means
to become a neighbor
       to those we may never have learned to know
       as friends.

And then there is the family we are born into.
Heavenly Father,
You see my own family,
      the little knot of this house,
daily struggle to understand
    what it means to be a family.
There are, obviously, cultural norms and expectations.
But I also believe there is,
      at the core of what "family" means,
something you plant in all of us:
a seed seeking good soil to grow
      in our fumbling to learn how to love
one another; to learn
        when to be lenient and when to be firm,
        when to demand and when to give in,
        when to insist upon our own needs
        and when to step aside for others;
what level of noise is acceptable;
what teasing is masked affection
        and when it tips into aggression;
how to be watchful of oneself and each other
      so to notice when enough is enough,
      when a hug may be needed, or a kiss,
      or when it's simply time to leave the room.

Every day, Lord, I watch my family
      struggle to be a family.
It can be exhausting, especially these days
      when we are so much together.
We all *want* to be together,
      but somehow one of us always in some way
needs to poke at the peace—and I find
we are like a squabble of seagulls on a mudflat:
      we go about our business peacefully enough until
      we take flight suddenly in one movement—
bickering, circling and
squawking at each other—before settling down again,
      shifting ruffled feathers back into place.

Some days it feels that more time is spent airborne
    than on the ground.
And yet, in the midst of the squabbling,
I sense we are trying to find ourselves, together,
    in you.
For you, Heavenly Father,
    are the love which binds us together.
And you are the love
    we want to express for each other,
        but often so awkwardly it seems like something else.
You are the love
    we need and seek in each other.
And you are the hope drawing us
    again and again into this hard work.

Holy Father,
it's hard to be a family.
All too often families break when,
either too easily
    or after long struggle,
they lose—or someone loses—
    hope—
and lose, therefore,
    sight of you;
and lose, therefore, the energy,
    tenacity and elasticity
of love.

Father,
we are your children.
In every widening circle of family
    to which we belong,
strengthen us, you who are Love,
    in the tenacity of love.
Teach us, you who are Forgiveness,
    to forgive one another.
Guide us in patience, you who are Wisdom,

  to know when to speak
    and when to be silent;
  when to insist
    and when to relent
and give in. Draw us, through our daily
    trials and errors,
until we find ourselves
    one family
     in you. Amen.

April 22
Easter Feria

For God so loved the world that he gave his only Son, so that everyone who believes in him may not perish, but may have eternal life. Indeed, God did not send the Son into the world to condemn the world, but in order that the world might be saved through him.

(John 3:16–17)

Loving Father,
this morning I awoke to rain,
    a wonderful, softening, April rain.
I remember last February, when we suffered
through six endless weeks of rain,
    my whole body yearned for sunshine and light.
I thought then that I could never welcome
    a day of rain again.
But today I awoke grateful for the rain.

I understand that my soul, like every living thing,
needs days of sunlight to grow,
    to be drawn out of itself,
        to spring forth with gladness, finding itself
        a ray of the universal light.
But I also need these days of rain—
    to settle, to be turned gently
    inwards, to be softened
    towards myself.

You send the spring rain to moisten the soil,
    to encourage roots, for Sabbath
    rest and gentleness,
    and humbleness of heart.
For the rain means forgiveness,

        patience, longsuffering, and mercy.
The rain, this Easter rain,
        my heart receives
as the love which does not condemn,
the love which falls to us, softening the earth,
        seeking what is hidden in it,
        preparing it,
encouraging us to open
        like germinating seed.

The rain, this Easter rain, falling,
my heart receives as a promise of compassion.
And today I believe I understand
        that to find peace in ourselves
            is to know your forgiveness;
that to be gentle with ourselves
        is to know your tenderness;
that to accept and love ourselves
        is to know your mercy.

Loving Father, in your providence
you give us days both of sunlight
        and of rain.
Sometimes, too much sun
        can harden us; too much light can wither us
and make us quick to judge—both ourselves and others.
        And then we need the rain.
Sometimes, too much rain
        saturates and muddies us, makes us complacent
and too much turned toward ourselves.
        And then we need the sun.

But today you have given me the rain.
And today, on waking to it,
        I understood I needed rain.
With the murmuring of the rain on the roof,
the world outside seems quiet.
And my heart is quiet.

And I am grateful.

Some days, you offer me the mercy
I'm not aware, before it comes,
      that I've been so much needing.
Today, though I call you "Father,"
I have needed the comfort
      of a mother.
I have needed, without knowing why,
the compassion of a mother—
her assurance that, no matter what,
      I am loved and, no matter what,
will never be turned away.
And today you have sent me rain.
And I am grateful.   Amen.

April 23
St. George, Martyr

The eyes of the Lord are on the righteous,
    and his ears are open to their cry.
The face of the Lord is against evildoers,
    to cut off the remembrance of them from the earth.

(Psalm 34:15–16)

Holy Lord,
today the psalmist compares the righteous
    with the wicked.
But who are the righteous,
    and who the wicked?
It seems to me that very few
    are truly wicked;
and very few
    might truly be called righteous.
Then there are the rest of us
    who are neither here nor there—
    ordinary sinners—
both those who cry out to you,
and those who, perhaps pulled away
    by the tides of the era's forgetfulness,
haven't ears enough to hear
    or apperception
of our need enough
    to whet their love.

That word, "righteous,"
    cannot mean "morally erect"—
    a pharisaical rectitude.
I believe it means the state of being
    in right relationship with you.
Your psalmist says your face is turned

    toward the righteous.
But do you turn your face to them because they please you,
    or is it because, first facing them,
     you draw to yourself the eyes
of their hearts
    and it is this that makes them righteous?

I have always thought of sin
    as a state of being
     in separation from you.
But do you turn away from the sinful because
    they first turn from you,
or is your turning from them
    the reason
they cannot see you—enough of you, at least,
    to seek you?

I know these are old questions
and that you have hidden the answers
    from our knowing.
But still, I need to ask.
    For it is by questions,
     and not by answers
that you lead me
    toward the quiet waters
of your word.

And there is always so much, my God,
    that I don't understand.

I don't understand, for example, why
you have set this desire for righteousness in me,
    this longing for life
     in relationship with you.
Why have you singled *me* out to prove
    your patience upon?
I have been aware, even as a child,
of your face turned towards me—

   though it took a long time
    and much kicking against the pricks,
for me to begin to perceive
that what you were offering was
   my life; that it was my own life
    you were holding out to me
and which I resisted with so much misplaced pride
   and adolescent obstinacy.

I remember, at twenty,
walking the wintry streets of Montreal,
distraught and wrestling with what I thought
   was my soul.
On arriving home, I announced,
   "I don't believe in God."
But the moment the words fell from my mouth
   I knew I was lying,
and that all my wrestling and hair-pulling
was play-acting and make-believe—
   though at the time I refused to admit it.
For I insisted on confusing my hair-pulling and play-acting
   with depth and with earnestness and life.

But all the while it was you, Lord,
   leading me through whatever barren
places through which
I needed to travel in order, finally,
 to turn
   and face you.
How is it, Lord, that you don't lose patience,
but seek again and again to turn my face
   and hold my gaze?
I don't understand—when there are so many
   in the same need,
    who desire life but don't know where to turn.
The only difference I can find
between them and me has nothing to do with
   me but only with your insistence.

Who, Lord, are the righteous?
Who are the unrighteous?
Perhaps you warn against judging others
    because the answer to that question
        is hidden so deeply in you.
For I am not aware that
        even my love for you
    is my own
and that even this is your precious gift
        to me, turning my face to yours.

I don't know why, Lord,
you keep me so patiently
    in your sight.
I don't often understand, Lord,
    what you are asking of me
    with your eyes.
I can do one thing only:
    respond with gratitude that it is me
you insist upon
    to love you.   Amen.

April 24

Martyrs of the Twentieth Century

One thing have I asked of the Lord, that will I seek after;
    that I may dwell in the house of the Lord
    all the days of my life;
to behold the fair beauty of the Lord
    and to inquire in his temple.

                                (Psalm 27:4, RSV)

Lord Jesus,
I pray today for your church of St. Barnabas,
    which I love.
I pray that you keep us whole and uplifted,
awake to your word for us now,
in this hour of our exile,
    and awake to one another,
so that we do not risk forgetting
    the gift you have given us in each other.

Lord Jesus,
especially now that we cannot gather together
    as the church
in the place we always knew to find you:
I pray that you keep us whole.

Bless all those you have given me to care for.

Not being able to gather,
not being able to give thanks
    or to eat together the food
        that nourishes and keeps us, together,
your body—
    makes everything and everyone
    seem so scattered. As if each

has gone his own way. Hold us
        together, Lord; feed us, your body,
when we have nothing with which
        to feed ourselves.

I remember a time
when I was too terrified and too proud
        to go to church:
terrified because I *knew*
    that to step across that threshold
        would change my life;
proud, because I was, at the same time,
disdainful of the people
        I assumed I'd find inside.

No one can accuse you, Lord,
        of lacking a sense of irony.
For this morning, when your church is locked down
        and your people isolated and scattered,
there is nowhere I would rather be
        than the place I was once too afraid
        to enter;
and there is no people with whom I would rather be
        than with those I was once too judgmental
        to join.

Lord Jesus,
today we read the story
of that time when, from a small boy's meager provision,
        you fed five thousand people.
All those people
had followed you into the wilderness
        on the far side of the Sea . . .
Miles from home, they grew hungry.
So, receiving the bread and the fish the boy gave you,
        you gave thanks, broke the bread,
        and gave it out:
more than enough for all those gathered

around you there,
>	those hoping to see and hear you,
>	those hoping to be touched by you
and healed.

The miracle is that you feed your church
>	when it comes to you
>>	empty handed.
You fed your people on a day you saw
>	danger of their drifting away
to look elsewhere for their food.

It had been such a long time
>	since they'd had a meal.

Lord Jesus,
Feed us, too—
>	your people, the little church of St. Barnabas.
It's been such a long time since we've gathered
>	around the table where you feed us
>	food
to sustain the life of your body.

Each day, Lord,
I come to you
>	with nothing to offer
but an empty heart
and a blank mind,
>	and only a morsel
of all you have given me
>	to offer.
I come to you with the fragment that I
>	am and that I have and each day
I go away with the bread of your Word
>	filling up my own.

Feed us, Lord Jesus,
with the food only you can give.
Feed us, for we are your body.   Amen.

April 27
Easter Feria

Then Jesus said to them, "Very truly, I tell you, it was not Moses who gave you the bread from heaven, but it is my Father who gives you the true bread from heaven. For the bread of God is that which comes down from heaven and gives life to the world." They said to him, "Sir, give us this bread always."

(John 6:32–34)

Lord Jesus Christ,
our pretensions are astonishing.
We believe we can be masters of nature
      when we can't even master ourselves.
We seek to control the whole realm of nature,
all the hidden strings of creation,
      and to make them serve *us*—
when we are constantly undone
      by the strings of our own hearts.

I was tired this weekend, Lord.
I don't know why, but I was on edge.
I got angry with Jasmin.
I don't know what set me off exactly,
      but the devil took advantage of my mood
      and I picked a fight with her.
I thought—if you can call it thinking—
I thought I needed to prove a point.
      But there was no point.
I just wanted to assert myself against her,
      assert power
    when I was feeling powerless.

Although we made up,
I still feel humiliated
        by my loss of self-control.
I regret that it happened.
But, aside from regret,
        there is another feeling in me too,
a feeling, Lord, which resists
     coming to light—
one I would prefer to keep hidden from myself
        and hidden from you.
It is a feeling almost like disappointment,
        that by losing control as I did,
by my puerile attempt to assert power,
     I *lost* power—
the power, maybe, of moral authority,
        (or perhaps *superiority*?)
which, before I lost my temper,
I believed, in my pride,
        was mine to wield between us?

Lord Jesus,
more than the fight or my loss of self-control,
I worry that this secret arrogance is
    the real sin
        you are bringing to light.

My God,
why do we lose our tempers?
Why do we even *have* tempers to lose?
You lost your temper,
        overturning the tables of the money-changers.
But then, you were protecting something
     you love.
Maybe that is what our anger is for:
to give us strength to safeguard
    what you have given us to love.
But why, then, do we turn our anger *against*
     those we love?

Why, instead of protecting something,
        does this snarling self-assertion
           sometimes set about destroying
everything?

Lord Jesus,
recalling my useless anger,
        I feel empty.
I offer it to you, this emptiness.
Please come and take it.
Forgive me my sins,
        both those I can and cannot see
           and especially those I try to hide
              from myself and you.
Forgive me, Lord,
        my anger, my self-assertion, my desire
for control over others when
        I cannot control even myself.

When I am impatient,
        give me patience.
When I am feeling empty, powerless,
        fill me with the power *not* to need
to prove myself
           over against others.
Give me peace with myself, enough
        to know that in your love I am
           so much more than I am.
Help me to acknowledge how little
        I am master even over myself,
           and do for me what I cannot:
turn my willful need to prove myself
        into occasions to prove your love;
take this emptiness I offer you
        and make in it a home for yourself—
so that I might find myself
        at home there too.   Amen.

April 28

Easter Feria

You stiff-necked people, uncircumcised in heart and ears, you are forever opposing the Holy Spirit, just as your ancestors used to do. Which of the prophets did your ancestors not persecute? . . . You are the ones that received the law as ordained by angels, and yet you have not kept it.

(Acts 7:51–53)

Spirit of God,
this morning we read the story
    of the stoning of Stephen.
Facing his accusers,
Stephen recounted their shared history—
the story of Abraham, Jacob, and Moses—
and he accused his accusers, the priests and elders,
    the appointed guardians of that story,
of not understanding what it said
    or where it led.
Hearing themselves accused,
they stoned him; and by doing so
    managed only to prove his words
true: they *themselves* made Stephen
    a prophet of your word.

Holy Spirit, Jesus himself promised
    that when we ask, you will
help us to understand the story in which
    we also play a part.

The chief priests and elders—we make caricatures
    of them and their stiff necks.
But I am also a priest of your church!

What were they committed to, after all,
	but protecting all they fervently believed
you had given them
		to love and protect:
			what they knew of your ways,
		their worship and their law,
their role in their community and in creation,
		where you had made for them
a special place.

If the story which Stephen told
		took root—would all of that not be in danger?
The story, as Stephen told it,
		did it not put the Temple—and everything
the Temple held and meant for them—
		at risk of destruction?

And so it was.

Spirit of God, the Temple priests,
		how blameworthy *were* they?
They were only defending what they knew
		to be your great gift to them:
the place your people went to seek and serve you,
		to worship and be renewed;
where they went to be reassured of your presence
		and your love for them.
No wonder they hated Stephen's take
		on their story!
How could they have suspected
		it came from you?

And I am also a priest of your church!

You place your priests to be lovers
	and guardians of your church (yes,
		even of the institution,
for there is no clean line dividing

    the spirit from the flesh).
But perhaps, in trying to guard and protect it,
    we end up undermining it.

Then again, in undermining it—crucifying Jesus,
    stoning Stephen—perhaps,
      in spite of ourselves,
we act as mid-wife as you labor to
    bring your church to birth!
Holy God! It is hard for us to trace
the voice of your Spirit's calling
    down the corridors of history—
      all the way here.

Yesterday I read the minutes
    of a missed clergy meeting in which
my colleagues toyed with the possibility of the diocese
    not returning to worship until the end
      of September.
The idea crushed me.
Why do I find the thought so hard?

Perhaps because I'm afraid, afraid of losing
    not only the church, but *myself*—
      my role in the story
in which I believe
  you have placed me
    to serve and to worship and to know
    myself in the part
you've given me to play.
I'm afraid because, where else but the church
can I empty my heart and yet find it—
    like the widow's jar of oil—constantly
full?

So rather than listen, rather than ask
    into what new thing may you be calling us?
I just want this whole ordeal

        to end, the sooner the better.
I want to return to the patterns
        and people you have given me
and who, at the same time,
        sustain me in every way.
Rather than listen, rather than ask,
        I find myself and my colleagues
scrambling to "do church" by every possible tool
we have at hand to prop up the falling
edifice we love; to continue,
        somehow just to continue
to serve in the ways we know
        sustain us.

Spirit of God,
my instinct, just like those priests of old,
is to get busy when what we love
        is threatened.
But maybe you are asking us just to
    stop for a moment,
stop and listen
        like Stephen listened for your unexpected
word, "at once
        so ancient and so new."[3]

Spirit of my Lord Jesus,
keep me from the fear which keeps me from listening.
Help me to hope for wherever it is
        you are leading us,
even if it's to places
        I don't think I want to go.

Teach me to love
        you, and not just that part of the story in which
I find myself but which you—
I cannot tell, Lord—
        you may be demanding
we must leave behind.   Amen.

April 29
Catherine of Sienna

And this is the will of him who sent me, that I should lose nothing of all that he has given me, but raise it up on the last day. This is indeed the will of my Father, that all who see the Son and believe in him may have eternal life; and I will raise them up on the last day.

(John 6:39–40)

Lord Jesus,
you are my God.
You are the love of all my loves,
      the joy of all my joys,
the one in whom I seek the hope
without which my life—
      all my small loves and joys,
      grievances and sufferings,
are for nothing.

Lord Jesus,
you are my God.
Your loving promise saves
      me and all I believe I live for—
   the truth and the goodness
      I cherish in all I love—
from nothing.

Lord Jesus,
You are my God.
You are the promise without which
   the purpose
      I have no choice but to believe
my life communicates—purpose
      I cannot see—is a lie.

You are the life which saves
my life from the dumbness of mere
    being: one among the numberless
shingle the tide drags up and down
the beach.

Lord Jesus,
You are my God
because I love my life
and, in loving it, am *unable*
        to conceive
it begins and ends
    in a lie.

Lord Jesus,
there are countless small joys
I delight in: joys of the birds
    and all the green and growing things;
joys of family and the pride I take
    in my children;
joys of the body; joys of the mind;
the sometimes almost sad joy
    in music and prayer and poetry;
joys of rough weather and of soft weather;
joys of work and of relaxation;
joys of a healthy exhaustion
    and of energy returning . . .
But if you do not raise them all,
if all that is good and beautiful,
    if all that gives me joy
falls into nothing—
    what then would my joy be?
Just a stretch of surface tension
    permitting me, perhaps, to stay,
    a while, afloat.

But the promise they hold out
> of a love that cannot die, would be
> a lie.

But *this is the will of him who sent me,*
> *that I should lose nothing*
> *of all he has given me*
>> *but raise it up.*

Lord Jesus,
you are my God
because you are the Joy
that makes all my joys
> Joyful;
and in your promise I begin
> to understand:
>> it is not that joy obscures
the reality of death,
but that death, when we forget you,
obscures the reality
> of Joy.

Lord Jesus,
you are my God.
In you, love and truth
> kiss each other.
Love, I see
> is the sense you give us
to waken our bodies,
to waken our minds,
> to what is yours.
To love is to be made
aware that what we love means
> more than it could ever mean to us;
that what we love is more
> precious than we can imagine;

that what we love is more loveable
>	than the love we are ever able to give
alone.

Lord Jesus,
you raise up our loves
and make them eyes of truth—
>	turning my small joys into windows opening
>	>	onto Joy.
Help me, Lord Jesus,
for you are my God,
>	help me to live
in the hope of your promise
>	to lose nothing of all that is yours,
>	and live
every day in the delight
of your eternal Joy.   Amen.

April 30
Marie de l'Incarnation

If I had cherished iniquity in my heart,
    the Lord would not have listened.
But truly God has listened;
    he has given heed to the words of my prayer.

                           (Psalm 66:18–19)

Lord Jesus,
every morning I begin
    my day with prayer.
I try to still myself
for a moment
    with your name on my lips;
to listen,
to open the door of myself enough
    for you to enter and sit for a while.

Some days
    when I pray I find you—
        or what I gratefully take to be you—
filling not my mind only, but almost
    the whole house!
Other days—at times days in a row—
I feel like an autumn leaf caught
    by a gust in a corner.

Even now, Lord,
I cannot say exactly
    why or what I hope for
    when I pray.

I know I long to be close to you.

Perhaps I pray
to give myself time to notice
  your presence already within me.
Or perhaps I pray to give myself
presence of heart to see that
  you are everywhere I look.
I cannot see you with my eyes,
so I must look for you
  with a different sense,
the sense you have given me
to look for you and find you—
 the sense you have taught me
 to think of as love.

That feels, at least right now,
 closer to the truth:
that I pray each morning to waken
the eyes of my heart
  so that I may think what I feel
  and feel what I think.
When I am awake in this way
it is as if my physical eyes also
  awaken—awaken and rejoice!
They rejoice, seeing your delight—
  in the candles just now blossoming
   on the chestnut outside my window;
    in everything life-giving and beautiful.
But they can also waken
  to your grief over what is ugly,
  the places you suffer with the suffering,
  the places from which we try to keep
love from entering.

It seems you give us the eyes of love,
Lord Jesus, to delight with you
  in what is delightful
and to grieve with you
  in what is grievous—

    as if giving us a small glimpse
(as much as we can bear) of the world
        as you behold it.

Lord Jesus,
when I pray it feels like I'm trying,
        bit by bit,
to open myself completely to you,
   to make myself transparent
        so there might be nothing between us,
nothing I am hiding
       from you or from myself.
I don't know where this need comes from,
but it is as if—if I could just become
        as clear as one of those glacier lakes—
        a clarity so clear that what looks like two feet
        is actually twenty feet to the bottom—
then I would belong to you completely;
then my whole life would be
        the prayer I long for it to be.

Perhaps, Lord, this is the cross
    you command us to carry:
that what we who love you
desire our life to be—
        a clear lake reflecting
        heaven's open sky—
we will receive only in death.
I don't know about this.
I only know that I long for there to be
       nothing between us
and that you will take away
        everything I put in the way.

Lord Jesus,
you told us to ask each day
        for our daily bread.
I ask for your presence.

I ask *to be* present.
I hope for love, to taste and see,
> to delight with you in the places of delight
> and grieve with you in the places of grief.
I ask for love's wisdom,
enough at least to take the next step
> on the road on which you wait for me, ahead.

Lord Jesus,
each morning, when I pray,
what I believe I am doing
> is asking you
to teach me how
> to pray—
and to make my whole life
> a word we share between us.   Amen.

May 1

St. Philip and St. James

Philip said to him, "Lord, show us the Father, and we shall be satisfied." Jesus said to him, "Have I been with you all this time, Philip, and yet you do not know me? He who has seen me has seen the Father; how can you say, 'show us the Father'?"

(John 14:8–9, RSV)

Lord Jesus, Christ Jesus,
Word of God, Son of God,
Lamb of God
      and Great Shepherd,
the Way and the Gate;
the Truth and the Life;
Icon of God, Glory of God,
Son of Man,
      Man of Sorrows . . .
Savior, Redeemer, Mediator,
Rock and Living Water,
Rabbi and Brother,
Bread of Life,
   Friend—

by what name am I to call you?
At the name of Jesus
      every knee should bow—but
you have so many names
      your name stretches us
beyond naming.

*Have I not been with you all this time,
Philip, and you still do not know me?*

But who *can* claim to know you, Lord?
Even though you give us
the whole of your whole self
        in every smallest crumb,
the whole of your whole kingdom
        in every smallest seed;
even though you give us to hold you
        in our outstretched palms,
it doesn't mean that we can hold you.
It means there is more
        in the smallest particle that is
    than is possible
for us to hold or comprehend:
        "the world in a hazelnut,"
        "infinity in the palm of our hand."[4]

Son of God,
if this is how you give yourself to us,
if every smallest thing that is
        contains all of you as
        you contain all things,
if everything that is
        is infinitely more
        than it is—
            my own small self included!
—then the world, this finite world,
we can only truly know
        without knowing but
in gratitude, love, and wonder.

Lord God, Lamb of God,
    I am afraid,
increasingly afraid we are forgetting
        how to wonder. I am
afraid of the world we are constructing,
a world in which every fish
        is counted,
every migrating bird

        mapped and managed,
a world in which nothing moves
        outside our say-so.

I am afraid how monitored
the world is, how regulated,
        claustrophobic; how we pace
up and down our
  allotted spaces
like a cougar in a cage with only
a dimming memory
        of forest;
or a salmon in a glass aquarium
slowly forgetting
        the sea.

Have I been with you all this time,
Philip, and still you do not know me?

Everything depends, Lord,
on the tone of your voice.
Is that exasperation?
Or are you beckoning Philip, calling,
coaxing him further
        on to see more and more—
infinitely more than there is for him
        to see?

Lord Jesus,
if I say I know you, then
        I do not know you.
But if I turn in wonder,
        if I turn in thanksgiving
toward you,
  then I am free
        to love and to know
that I am
        known by you.

Remind us, Lord Jesus, how to know
        not to know—
so that we may know you in faith
        and be free.   Amen.

May 4
Easter Feria

For thou art the God of my strength; why hast thou put me from thee?
*   and why go I so heavily, while the enemy oppresseth me?*
O send out thy light and thy truth, that they may lead me,
and bring me unto thy holy hill, and to thy dwelling.

                            (Psalm 43:2–3, BCP)

Our Father, who art in heaven,
    I believe
  it was Brother Lawrence
who told of an old monk who,
      kneeling down each morning
        to say the Lord's Prayer,
never managed to get any further
than the words "Our Father"—
so full did he find them
      of everything he meant
        and of everything he hoped,
and of all that he could possibly need
      for the day.

In my clearest moments, Father,
I understand that old monk.
   It is as if, when
I have been able properly
      to attend to the words
        your Son has given us,
when I opened my mouth,
when I opened my self
      to address you,
I found you
      have already filled my words.

In my clearest moments,
I have shared that old monk's
       simplicity: shared his fear,
his amazement and thanksgiving and joy
in finding you
     have gone before me, anticipating me,
        filling my words with your word
        even before I begin to speak.

Father in heaven,
and not *my* Father only,
       but *Our* Father—Father of all people,
Father of all that exists
       in heaven and on earth:
even this first thought
       is much too much for me.
You are at one and the same time
       the most intimate
       and the most universal.
You encourage me to turn to you—
       the small bundle of cares
        and hopes and dreams that I am—
and yet I am nothing
    more or less
than any one of the billions of beings
       now living, or the billions more
who are now dead, or—and who knows?—
       perhaps, in your eternal light,
the billions more who are
    yet to be.
That thought, when I try to hold it,
       terrifies me. It risks annihilating me
        by a kind of vertigo.
How can I matter to you?
How can I hold your attention
       or be anything more than a number,
    a statistic, one molecule
among the numberless

molecules buzzing on the surface of the earth?
How can I mean more to you
    than nothing?

Yet you count every grain of sand,
and every hair on every head.
You contain everything that is—
    and in such a way that you bid each thing
to call you "Father,"
    each in in its own way,
each in the language you have given
    it to speak: bird and lily,
    grain of sand, star in the night sky,
and even me, who you have given to pray.

Heavenly Father,
you know better than I do
    that I cannot live
if I do not have a place
  in your house, a place
    in your heart.
When you reassure me that I am
    your child,
when you bid me to speak to you as my Father,
and assure me therefore of my place
    in your house
    and that I am
counted and valued and cherished
    and named;
when you assure me that I am loved—
   you give me life
    and sustain me in my being.

Our Father in heaven.
I cannot see you
    though you are
everywhere sustaining each thing in its way
as you are sustaining me

      in mine.
It makes me fearful when I try to imagine
      how you attend to each thing
with the very same attention
      with which you attend to me.
But I am grateful, Father,
    more grateful than these words
of thanks can mean,
      for my life
      and for the life
of the whole world.   Amen.

May 5
Easter Feria

My sheep hear my voice. I know them, and they follow me. I give them eternal life, and they will never perish. No one will snatch them out of my hand.

(John 10:27–28)

Father,
your name is Holy:
> *Holy, Holy, Holy,*
> *Lord God of hosts.*
Not only the angels,
but the whole multitude
> of your creatures gathers
in their being to praise
and to give you thanks.
> *Heaven and earth are full*
of their voices singing
> *of your glory.*
Of your goodness
> they sing, and of your holiness,
all things lifting the song
> of their being
as I am lifting mine
> to you now.

For how could I live, Holy Father,
> if it were not for your goodness?

In the shallows of my thought,
> where I sometimes plash and
toy with possibilities,
I try to imagine
> that there is nothing
> > like your goodness;

that the universe contains nothing
        that is good
in itself; that therefore neither
        is there any evil,
but that there is only
what we *call* good—
        what benefits us—
and what we *call* evil—
        what does us harm;
and that it is possible to carry on
        in a world and with a life
empty of any promise
        of abiding goodness.

But as soon as I swim
        out from the shallows,
as soon as I can no longer
      see bottom, I become fearfully
aware that I cannot
        live, flourish, strive, hope
if I cannot, in the depths,
        be assured—
assured beyond utility,
beyond self-affirmation,
beyond the congratulation of others,
beyond even conscious thought,
      that I am not good only for nothing
but that I am
        good.

Where can I look, Holy Father,
for the goodness
        that is the air and water
     and the bread
I need to live
        if I cannot look to you?

When I pray,
when I come to myself,
I know I really know only one thing:
  that you are the ground
without which I cannot walk;
  that you are the air
without which I cannot breathe;
  that you are the ocean
in which I swim;
  that without you,
nothing is good;
  that without you, *therefore*
  nothing can be.

And so it is just by their being
  and their being alive
that all things praise
  and stretch toward you.
For in their desire to live
  and to propagate, to flourish
  and to grow,
each creature in its way—
  even the wood bug under the rotting board—
is a song of praise
  for your goodness.

Holy, Holy, Holy Lord,
Heaven and earth are full
  of your glory . . .

Holy Father,
I know that there is also much evil
  in the world,
that there is much that distorts
  the perfect clarity
  of your holiness.
But let me not be concerned
  with that today.

Perhaps tomorrow,
but today let me praise you
      with an untroubled heart.
For today I know,
 beyond every good and every evil,
      you alone are the Holy One,
      you alone are the Lord.
Today I praise you with
      my lips
and I praise you with
      my breath
and I praise you with
      the wholeness of my whole life.
I praise you because I am
and because you are
      the goodness of all
      that is good;
and the holiness of all
      that is holy.   Amen.

May 6

St. John the Evangelist

This is the message we have heard from Jesus Christ and proclaim to you, that God is light and in him there is no darkness at all.

(1 John 1:5)

Our Father, who art in heaven,
Hallowed be thy name
Thy Kingdom come,
Thy will be done on earth
As it is in heaven.

Father,
I can't imagine heaven.
When others speak to me
      of how they imagine heaven,
   and how it will be, one day,
when they arrive,
I often feel awkward.
I am their pastor—and I know
      they look to me to share
      their hope, share in the joy
of their hope, and in sharing
confirm it. But I can't.
Simone Weil wrote
"We cannot take a step
toward the heavens. God crosses the universe
and comes to us."
T.S. Eliot bid us
      to "wait without hope, for hope
      would be hope for the wrong thing;"
and St. John of the Cross said,
      "to arrive at being all,
      desire to be nothing."[5]

I think they mean to encourage us
> to trust you to the point
> of blindness—
seeing nothing, knowing
> nothing, imagining nothing but giving
> our future, ourselves, our hope
> for ourselves entirely into your
unimaginable hands.

Holy Father,
that may be the meaning of faith
> and the task of love—
the task of giving ourselves entirely
> up to you
as you gave yourself up entirely
> for us in Jesus.
But that task,
> if it is the task,
 is too hard for me.
It seems too much like suffering.
I'm too attached, Lord,
> to let go of who
I imagine myself to be
and all the cherished dreams
> that go along with who
> I want so badly to believe
> that I am.
So when I pray, "Thy will be done,"
for whose future—yours or mine—
> am I truly praying?

Perhaps, Father,
I think too much about
> what I think.
I remember, one recent summer,
a day I spent grieving,
frustrated that time and age and circumstance
were impelling me to relinquish

        hopes long treasured—
dreams that always seemed to be
           an essential part of what I believe
           is me.
I remember, it was at Roberts Creek,
lying on my back in the grass and looking
           up into the crown of a single
           tall Douglas fir growing
        at the edge of the field.
There it was:
     imperfect and disproportioned
and yet so sharply set against
        the blue sky
it appeared almost cut out
    of the surrounding space,
      so perfectly
        perfectly itself.

I thank you, Father,
for that moment
        of grace. Looking,
      I saw
I was—that my life was—
        that tree. Looking,
I knew you held me
       as you held it,
your light making perfect
        something so misshapen
and yet also
        so strong, so entirely delivered
        to be itself.

Heavenly Father,
more happened in that moment
        than I can explain.
I cannot imagine heaven.
But when I pray
    Thy will be done,

I remember how the light
        held that tree.
I remember that you have given me
        something to remember beyond
        my memory; something
to see, to hear beyond
        my understanding.

I pray, when I pray
      Your will be done on earth,
        for the world to be
        held in the light in this way,
a way I cannot imagine,
        this way in which you have given me
to hope
        for what I cannot hope.   Amen.

May 7
Easter Feria

I will sing of your steadfast love, O Lord, forever;
    with my mouth I will proclaim your faithfulness to all generations.
                                                        (Psalm 89:1)

Our Father, who art in heaven,
every day I pray
        Thy will be done.
But the thing I especially want to know is
        "What *is* your will?"
What is your will for me?
What is your will for us—
            for our parish?
            for your whole church?
            for your whole world?

When I think carefully about it,
it seems that when I ask,
        "What is your will?"
I mean one of two things.
Sometimes I am wanting
        to know the path I ought to take,
        the answer to a choice I have to make,
to see plainly the way
        you providentially map out for me . . .

Yet, when I ask, "What is your will,"
        more than *your* will,
if I am honest, what I really want to know is
        what will best fulfill
the inchoate hope
        I hold for myself and
  make me happy.

When I ask,
> "What is your will?"

it is in truth for my *own* happiness I'm asking—
in the hope, or perhaps the expectation,
that they *must* be the same:
> that your will for me and my happiness
> must be the same.

Is this impertinent of me, Father?

More often, though, when I ask,
> "What is your will?"

I am asking for concrete direction
either for myself or for the people and things
> for which you have given me

responsibility; I am needing
> concrete direction amid
> concrete circumstances,

whatever they may be.

In both situations, Father,
when I ask, "What is your will?"
> I see I'm asking you
> > to show me what I should do.

But, Father, I have noticed,
> or at least it has been my experience,

that you answer this kind of prayer, directly,
> only very rarely.

Once you led a friend I prayed for
> to baptism. Once,

before I even knew, at least consciously,
> *how* to pray, you called—or pushed me—

toward the priesthood.

Holy Father, I'm sure
it can't be wrong to ask,
> "What is your will?"—

for you love us and hold
> our cares to your breast.

And I am sure you move us
        in many ways we cannot see.
But perhaps it is just *because*
        you love us
 that you withhold
        clear answers from us.
Perhaps you already said
        all that is necessary and needed
when Jesus said:
        I give you a new commandment,
        that you love one another.
        Just as I have loved you,
        you should love one another.

There may be many paths
open to us,
        or there may be relatively few;
there may be many decisions before us,
many responsibilities to weigh,
        or there may be relatively few.
Nevertheless, Father,
   I believe you
        to have said there is only one
 path—and that is love's path;
and there is only one decision—
        and that is love's decision;
and there is only one responsibility—
        and that is to love.
Love is your commandment,
your promise, and your will—and then,
after we have understood this,
        it seems, for the most part,
you leave the details to us.

Father, it sounds simple,
   but why is it so hard to know
what path is love's path,
what decision is love's

        decision? It leaves
everything so uncertain when
        what we really seek from you is certainty.
But certainty, it seems,
    is precisely what you withhold.
Instead, what you offer us
is faith.

Heavenly Father,
the freedom you give us,
        love's freedom, is hard.
Help us
        to love as you love us.
Help us, Father,
        to be free enough,
        free from our own will
enough, to pray
        Thy will be done.   Amen.

May 8

Julian of Norwich

Jesus said to him, "I am the way, and the truth, and the life. No one comes to the Father except through me. If you know me, you will know my Father also."

(John 14:6–7)

Father in heaven, I realize
how self-concerned my prayers
      tend to be; how often
when I turn to you I turn
      inwards.
I'm not entirely sure that that's
      unfitting,
for I'm not sure how to begin
if not with myself:
      "I shall look for you, Lord, by praying to you
      and as I pray, I shall believe in you . . ." [6]

Nevertheless, perhaps this only goes
to show how much of a beginner
      I really am. For today I noticed
that *before* Jesus bids us to pray
      "give us this day our daily bread,"
he says to pray
      "your will be done on earth"—

The *whole* earth, Father.
I am to pray not only for my own
      good, my own
loves, my own world of people
      and concerns,
but I am to pray for the whole
earth, leaving myself, as it were, out
      of the equation.

Is there space and time
    enough for us all
without destroying what we love?
If I pray for the goods
    I believe belong to me, how
do my desires clash with the cries of others?
I'm afraid of what you need to take away
    from me so that others may receive
    their share.
Help me, Father, to pray for the good
    that does not seem good to me:
the good of the whole earth
    without regard to my own
good; the life of the whole
earth, without regard to my own
    life; the future of the whole
earth, without regard to the hopes
    I harbor for my own future.

Holy Father, your rain falls
    on the just and unjust alike.
How might we perceive
    the needs of the earth
if we didn't always need to look
    through the lens of our need?
Or how might we perceive
    the good of the earth
if we didn't always look
    through the lens of our own desire?—

Even when I pray for justice
on the earth, I see it's almost impossible for me
    not to place myself
    on the side of the just.
And even when I ask forgiveness,
it is, after all, something for myself
    that I'm asking for.

But how, Holy Father, would I perceive
        your will for the earth
if I could escape from myself
        and listen with ears not my own?

I am tempted sometimes
by a kind of quietism—as if whatever
        happens on earth happens
only because it is your will.
Something like this thought appears, at times,
     in the Bible:
        "Let every person be subject to the governing
          authorities. For there is no authority except from God,
          and those that exist have been instituted by God."
But that voice seems at odds
with a more urgent voice:
        "Hear, O heavens, and listen, O earth;
   for the Lord has spoken:
        I reared children and brought them up
   but they have rebelled against me."

Father, even in our time,
when it's not so hard to hear
        the whole earth groaning,
who can speak,
who has authority to speak,
        with that more urgent voice
proclaiming your will
        for the earth?
You know I have wanted, Lord,
        that I have been tempted to want,
to speak in that way.
But there's such a cacophony of warring
words out there—opinions
        and words—how can we know
if the word we *would* speak is not just another
        word thrown
  onto that high heap of words,

but a true word of your one Word?

I believe, Father,
that there is work you send us
to do. But I wonder if that work,
the work of welcoming joy in the midst
        of suffering, I wonder whether
that work does not begin
    by the imperative to speak
in love for what we love
        but then, before we speak,
emptying our love
        of every shadow
of self-
        inflection?
I wonder whether, to welcome
        joy in the midst of suffering,
we must be willing to let you
        take from us our prayer for the goods
we believe life ought to deliver to us?

I wonder if something like this
is what Jesus meant when he said
        "I am the Way, the Truth, and the Life.
        No one comes to the Father except
  through me?"

Help us, Father, to hear your Word
        for the earth.
Help us to pray *your will*
        be done on earth before
we pray for your will
    for ourselves.   Amen.

May 11
Easter Feria

The Lord has been mindful of us; he will bless us;
  he will bless the house of Israel;
he will bless the house of Aaron;
  he will bless those who fear the Lord,
both small and great.

(Psalm 115:12–13)

Your will be done
  on earth as it is in heaven.

Thank you, Father,
for the past two days—
  especially for the soft
    early mornings—soft
with the sense
  of waiting
for something: the hush
  before the curtain rises,
the lush readiness that is like
  wonder.

Attempting to imagine
what "on earth as in heaven"
might be—this may be as close
as I get: the breathless
  expectation—which even the trees
seem to take part in—
  of new life coming over the lip
    of the horizon.
But no doubt, Father, this
says more about me
  than about you.

Yesterday, for Mothers' Day,
    the family rafted down the Cowichan River,
        fishing, but mostly just floating.
Since we couldn't all fit in Tristan's raft,
I went along beside
    in the pontoon boat: perfect,
since although we were all together,
it gave me time to be
    alone with my thoughts, drifting
under canopies of newly-leaved
    maples and a milky sky.
It was the kind of day I love best,
    and the kind of day
        our family needed:
a day together but in which
there seemed space enough
for each of us to be
    happy in his
or her own way.

As I floated on the river,
Father, as my heart gave thanks
    for the day,
I wondered why I so often feel,
    amid even times of special
    contentment,
a kind of desperate need to collect
    the moments of
        my life
as if they are pieces
    of a complicated jigsaw puzzle.
Why do I feel the necessity
    to collect them and piece
    them together?
Why feel the necessity for there to be
    somewhere a key showing
        me how they fit together

        so that I don't lose them,
so that they hold in place,
so that I can see
        they make a picture—
            one which,
when it is finished, I will wonder
        at and say "Yes!
That is who I am! That is me."

Father, you know this
        desperation because, for the life of me, I can't—
        hold on to the time
and to the moments.
    They slip past.
I keep dropping pieces.
Long stretches just don't seem
        to fit anywhere . . .

Father, if everything slips
away like this; if I can't hold on
        even to the shape of one
perfect tree—one perfect
        moment—let alone
        a whole landscape of passing
moments, what is it for?
What is the day for?
   —the beauty of the day,
the love we share,
these particular eyes through which
        I drink in the world and whose gaze
seems so infinitely precious to me,
    giving rise to feelings and thoughts
so infinitely important to me
because they are so completely
        inseparable from me and
who I am.

Father, I believe,
>   although imperfectly,
I do believe, at those times when
>   you free me from myself, that it's all
>   for praise: every moment is
a moment to praise you
>   and in praising you
offer it back
>   to you for safekeeping.
As I live, moment to moment
>   on the earth, you store up for me
>   my life in heaven.
Is that not, after all, the place
>   you are preparing for me?
So that, on the day
>   I finally lose myself utterly,
I will find myself
>   waiting, perfect and complete.
I will find that I am
>   waiting for myself
> on that day, with you,
there.   Amen.

May 12
Florence Nightingale

Peace I leave with you; my peace I give to you. I do not give to you as the world gives. Do not let your hearts be troubled, and do not let them be afraid.

(John 14:27)

Our Father, who art in heaven,
    Give us this day our daily bread . . .

My life is not like
the lives of so many who
    live day to day
        only on what they scrape
that day together;
those who know their families
that day will eat only what
    the day provides.
I have seen the slums
    of Calcutta and I think
of those who live in them
and who have been told, as we have,
    to shut down, to stay at home,
but who must hear this as
    a starvation order.
What does "shut down" mean
    to them?
What do the words
Give us this day our daily bread
    mean?

I don't want, Father,
    to presume anything
about the thoughts

of those whose lives are so
    radically different from my own,
but how can those words *not*
    mean for them something
far different than they mean
    for me?

Give us this day our daily bread.
I wonder, Father, if that's the reason
    Jesus said it's easier for a camel
to pass through the eye of a needle
than for a rich man to enter
    the kingdom of God:
because the rich man—
    such as I am—
cannot pray for his daily bread
with the same urgency as the man
for whom this prayer must be
    as urgent as his desire
for life,
    and whose dependency
    on what he can't foresee
isn't softened by a bank account, steady
employment, or a fridge full of food.

Father, you know I have always known
    what it means to have
more than enough of everything
    I need:
not only food, but more than enough
opportunity and encouragement
    and ability.
I have always known what it is
    to be loved.

Father—are all these riches I've enjoyed
    not blessings that every one
of your children should know

    and *would* know if the world
     were just; and
if your kingdom would come
    on earth?

Yet I am also aware of something
    else—aware
by the fact that I don't know
    (and I mean "know" by an ache
    in my belly) exactly
what I pray for when I pray
for my daily bread
    (and I mean "pray" as if my life
    depended on your answer).
I am aware, however ungrateful
    this may seem,
    that all my blessings
have trapped me in
    another kind
of poverty.

When you have eaten your fill
and have built fine houses . . .
And your silver and gold is
multiplied, and all that you have is
multiplied, then do not
exalt yourself, forgetting
the Lord your God . . .

Heavenly Father,
I am aware—aware as I am
    sometimes of stars
I can see only from the corner
    of my eye, stars that, when
I turn to look at them directly,
    disappear from view—
I am aware, Father,
of a poverty in me:

the poverty of a world
        so exalted
        in surfeit
that it has forgotten
        you.

I am aware, Father,
that the world lives in me
        even more, perhaps, than
I live in it.
    I pray, "Give us this day
our daily bread" but
        I don't live in
daily thanksgiving
for the day's sustaining
        grace.

I cannot pray for poverty, Father.
You know I am nowhere
        near ready for that.
But I pray at least for what
        I believe I really do want:
a meetly urgent
        gratitude when I receive,
as I always do receive,
        from your hand,
my daily bread.   Amen.

May 13
Easter Feria

If you abide in me, and my words abide in you, ask for whatever you wish, and it will be done for you. My Father is glorified by this, that you bear much fruit and become my disciples.

(John 15:7–8)

Our Father, who art in heaven,
    Give us this day our daily bread . . .

In the time of his temptation, Father,
    when Jesus isolated
himself to look for you and
    for himself: during the time
of his temptation, when
    he was famished—
famished the moment
    he'd begun to understand
        the power which was his:
when the tempter tempted him,
    inviting him to satisfy first
his own hunger, Jesus said:
    "one does not live
        by bread alone, but by every word
        that comes from the mouth of God . . ."
For he is himself
    the word and the bread
    of heaven.

You know, Father, just how much hunger
there is in me—far more
    hunger than the hungers
of the body, blunt
    and persistent as those are.

For one, I am hungry, Father,
        for *experience*: instead of being
satisfied by the bounty
        of the day, it's as if I want
        to devour the world.
It's as if seeing is a kind of eating,
as if, when I gaze on something beautiful—
        a particular tree, the sky at dusk—
I want to eat it, to take it all
        into myself . . . or maybe what I want is
to be swallowed
    by the beauty that I see.

I'm hungry, Father, also for
        adventure: instead of knowing
peace in the simple
        and daily round
of things you have given me to tend,
I find that I'm restless,
ambitious—not for wealth, but
    for experiences I dream will catapult
    me out of the everyday—
as if there's not miracle enough
        in every ordinary thing.

I'm hungry too, for
the affirmation
    that feeds my need to be seen,
to be valued as somehow
        unique.
I have a fear of crowds.
Father—I dislike
        them because in a crowd,
in the city,
my sense that I, too, am a pearl of great
        price, my sense
that I, too, am visible, that I, too,
        could possibly be

loved, begins to wear thin; and I experience
a lurch in my gut as if
   peering over the roof-edge
   of a tall building.

But I've also the need
   to give thanks,
   to praise you, Holy Father,
to sing in my way, and to create.
  I have a need for affection,
a need to give and to receive
   love and the mutuality
   of friendship.
I hunger for understanding
   and to make sense of things.
I desire also a kind of purity
   of mind and soul. I desire
   holiness—though I'm a little
embarrassed to admit it, it seems
so out of keeping
   with the world.

Father, you see
   how much hunger there is
in me. It's bewildering, how all these
  desires swarm together
in unaccountable
   variations. It's no wonder that Jesus,
after instructing us to pray
for our daily bread, instructed us to pray
   not to be led into temptation.

However numerous
   the desires that buzz about in me,
I think, Father, they all come down
to one: the desire for
   life, for abundance
   of life.

All my desire, Father,
        and perhaps even the desire for
death is meant to serve life
        and therefore meant
           to serve you.
For you are the Way and the Life
        of my life.
I love so many things, Holy Father,
but it is always you who move me,
        for you are love itself.

Holy Father, when I pray
        give us this day our daily bread,
help me both to see
        the true bread that feeds
me, and also so to
     discipline my hunger
that, rather than being scattered away,
        I am led daily to your word
        with which alone you fill me
with the bread of life.   Amen.

May 14
St. Matthias

O Lord, who may abide in your tent?
    Who may dwell on your holy hill?

(Psalm 15:1)

Our Father, who art in heaven
    forgive us our trespasses.

I know, Lord, of many sins,
both recent and past,
sins for which I ask
    your forgiveness:
I have lost my temper
    with my wife and my children;
I have been, at least inwardly,
   impatient with others;
I have been judgemental
and have not always sought
    first to see the good in others;
I have what once were called
    carnal thoughts—and have allowed
myself to forget to practise
    stewardship of my eyes;
I have coveted, even if gently,
opportunities granted to others—
    especially some which greater wealth makes
    possible for them;
I have been inattentive at prayer;
I have not been alert
   or responsive
    enough to the needs of others . . .

In and of itself, Lord,

I cannot feel this list too
        egregious. To it I am sure you
could add much more; but all
these sins seem such ordinary,
        such very human, things.
It might be easy to forgive
myself for them—if I didn't
        remember they are signs
of something else: how easy it is
        to put you aside;
how easy it is
        to compromise my conscience;
how easy it is to be so reconciled to living
separated from you that my actions are often
        sharp shrugs of non-committal.

Each one of these in-themselves
        likely insignificant
sins, I am reminded, Father, are signs
        of a deeper restlessness—and
that restlessness is a sign
        of a still deeper anxiety—and that
that anxiety is a sign of what
        really is
at stake between me and you:
that there is a void
        in my life, in my
faith an abyss
        I cannot cross myself
over to you.

I know, Father, the gift
        you've planted in me.
But I also know that this hope,
this faith and
        this love is only the tiniest seed
        of what *would* grow
if only I could

        let it grow.
I stand before
        a door I long to go through: a door
leading into the freedom that moves
        mountains. But something
stops me, weighs against me—a blind
intransigence pushing from
        the other side.
Father, where does that weight
        come from? Does it come from some dark
corner of my own soul?
Is it the world's grip,
        or Satan's grip, on me?

Wherever it comes from,
        I do not understand my own actions.
        For I do not do what I want
        But do the very thing I hate.
But what, Lord, is it, then, that
I want, but cannot, do?
Lord, you know that I love you.
    I want to love you.

Jesus said to us,
        "if you love me, then keep
        my commandments."
And it is just here, Father,
that you make the gulf
        separating my intention
from my reality
        visible.
For what did he command?
    "Deny yourself, and pick up your cross."
    "Go, sell all you have, and give
the money to the poor."
    "Love your neighbor as yourself."

If I love you, Lord, as I believe I do,
    why can't I do what you ask?
It's as though I'm so paralyzed
I don't even know how
       to begin . . .
If I loved you,
if I trusted you,
    if you were, as
I say you are *everything to me*,
would doing these things not be
as natural as waking
       and eating and
breathing?

Lord, forgive me my trespasses.
Help me to know how to begin
       to obey you, to love
you until
    you are to me
        everything.   Amen.

May 15
Easter Feria

This is my commandment, that you love one another as I have loved you. No one has greater love than this, to lay down one's life for one's friends.

(John 15:12–13)

Our Father, who art in heaven,
>   forgive us our trespasses as we forgive
>   those who trespass against us.

It is clear, Father,
that when your Son gave us these
>   words by which to approach you,
he was at the same time teaching
us about ourselves: that we are
first and foremost
>   what we love: worldly
when we love the world; human
when we love humanity; godly
when we love God.

He taught us to pray,
>   our Father,
for forgiveness for all
>   the ways we turn
our back on you; the ways
>   we turn from life by seeking life,
>   in our confusion,
>   in death.
But another thing for which
he taught us to pray
>   is strength of heart—or rather
>   *weakness* of heart
to forgive those who hurt us

as you forgive
>   those who hurt
you.

Forgiveness, he taught us,
>   is your Spirit's
>   gift: for it requires
>   the same grace,
the same strength of
>   weakness not our own,
that Jesus drew on
>   on the Cross.
To forgive is to be strong
>   in your weakness; it is
>   to empty ourselves
of our right to justice
in order for another kind of
>   justice to arise: resurrection
justice, the justice of
your kingdom,
>   come.

When Jesus taught us to pray,
he taught us to pray,
>   our Father,
for the strength to follow him
>   in the way of weakness,
>   the weakness of the cross.
But he also taught us that
just as no one sins
>   alone, so no one forgives
alone, and to forgive is to
>   disclose: your coming
Kingdom, Father,
>   is more real
than the reality
>   of the world. So I will wait
for you, Father,

       I will wait
for your resurrection
          justice, believing I will
understand *then* the justice of
all in all in
Christ.

Just as I seek to forgive,
Father, those who've hurt me
I will seek the forgiveness of those
    I've hurt—
and if they are unable, as
       I, too, have been unable
to forgive, then that
      is a cross
       I must carry—and that, too,
is a way I'm pledged to wait
for you.

We are plunged,
from the beginning, into
      a world
of sin and you call us, Father,
from the beginning, to understand that
darkness is
       stronger than we are but
not stronger than the light
   of your coming
day: the grace to live
in the long morning's shadow cast
       over the world by
the cross.

Lord, this body of death
is both mine and not mine,
       for I inherited it. And yet
you say that I am
       answerable for the sin

of the world which lives
in me and in which
      I live.
Help me, Father,
to be strong enough
    to be weak enough
to forgive and *thus* to
      wait
for the day of
      resurrection when
all hurt is
      forgiven and
all returned to all
      and all
will understand.   Amen.

May 18

Rogation Day

You visit the earth and water it,
      you greatly enrich it;
the river of God is full of water;
      you provide the people with grain,
      for so you have prepared it . . .
You crown the year with bounty.

                                    (Psalm 65:9, 11)

Holy Father,
everything we have comes
      from your hand.

I am sure it once was
      easier, more intuitive for people
to understand this than
      it is for us now.
They had to wait
for the rain and wait for the sun;
they planted then
      waited in prayer—
for they knew it was you
      who put life
      in the seed so that it would
sprout and grow and
      return thirty-fold, sixty-fold,
a hundred-fold according
      to the seasons
of your will.

But now we find it irritating
just to be made to wait to enter
      the grocery store.

When everything comes so easily,
       it makes it hard
           to understand why
    we must wait.
When we are so far
       removed from the seed
and the soil; when even
the "agricultural sector" is just another
international conglomerate and no longer
       a sacred communion,
a ritual of offering and
       receiving, of blessing
and thanksgiving—that is to say,
       an act of *Eucharist*, it makes it
hard to understand,
in the immediacy of our bodies,
       that all things come
from you.

Holy Father,
today is a Rogation
       Day—a day the Church,
from ancient times, sets
       aside to give thanks
for the planting and to ask
your blessing on the seed
       and to begin
          to wait for the grace
upon which our life
       and every life
depends.

Today is also the eleventh birthday of
    my son, Matthias.
It seems a fitting
       day to celebrate,
giving thanks for the wonderful
       life that is in him:

his enthusiasm for adventure;
his love for people and his kindness;
his love for animals
    and the hidden things
        he finds under rocks on the beach;
for his imagination at play;
for his talent for finding trouble and his
        grief when he does;
for his fearlessness for himself.

Holy Father,
all things come from your hand.
I thank you for Matthias,
    who is your gift.
Once, before he came to
our family, we didn't even know
    that we were waiting
for him, or how much our family
needed him. But now
    we do.

Yesterday, in the pouring
    rain, we went mushroom picking:
and there was Matthias
    shimmying gleefully up the dead alders
to get at the shelves of mushrooms out
    of his reach.
We came home drenched but
happy, baskets laden
    with oyster mushrooms
and with hearts full
of nothing we mentioned but
    with untroubled knowledge of our
having been together: the fresh green
of the woods; the little flowers
along the path; the unfurling
sword ferns; communion together in
    the gift of all we are

given—and for which
  our life is
this offering of praise
      and thanksgiving.   Amen.

May 19

Rogation Day

Restore our fortunes, O Lord,
 like the watercourses in the Negeb.
May those who sow in tears
 reap with shouts of joy.

(Psalm 126:4–5)

Our Father, who art in heaven
 Lead us not into temptation...

Holy Father,
you make me a work of your hand.
You raise me from nothing
 and stamp your living
image upon the dust
 that I am.
What does it mean to be
 led into temptation?
Does it mean for our eyes—
 eyes you created to look
outwards—to be drawn rather
inwards to look, first and
 foremost, to ourselves?
Does it mean for our ears—
ears you gave us to waken
 to the world around
us—to be tuned instead to our own
 clamoring voices?
Is to be tempted to
 be confused?
To love something in a way
 which is not love; to desire
the wrong thing—what is not

        meant for us—
or to desire the right thing
    in the wrong way?

When I feel myself
tempted, Lord, it seems
        I confuse
freedom with hunger.
It seems I begin to see
          your creatures—and even my own
self—almost as food for
        my own feeding
           instead, in the first place, as gifts
        to be lifted up to you
for blessing.

I don't know, Father,
        if *you* lead me
into temptation, but
I do know you bless
        the world with so much
beauty, so much that is
lovely, so much that I want but
        which is not for me
to touch. And you bless
the world with so much that is
good, but which is
        not good for me
to have. Yet I am
to delight in them still.
I am to delight in and for
        those for whom they are
given. I am to delight
in them just
        because they are
not mine but
yours.

For I know, Father,
that you apportion
      me my own
        share in your goodness.
Is it your fault
that I forget, that I tire
      of myself, that
I begin to feel your always-
particular, always-
      concrete gifts as
chains rather than
      wings; that I confuse, again
and again, *hunger* for the promise
      of freedom
and my neighbor's wife
      for abundance of life?

Jesus said,
    "Consider the lilies of the field,
    how they grow—even Solomon
    in all his glory was not clothed
    like one of these . . ."

Why, Father, do I find
it so hard to be
      like the lily,
who makes the field radiant,
whose existence is,
      perfectly, just
in the beauty you have given
      her to be hers?
Why is there so much
restlessness in me, Father?
Why can't I be
      at peace as
the lily is at peace?
Why must our hunger
take us to intrude at tables where

    no place is set for us?

Each day's portion seems just
    too paltry a meal to fill me—
all that I am, this infinite
hope that I am, this endless
    horizon of promise. How can
this day's gift possibly add up
    to enough? This house? This wife?
These boring streets? This job? How can this small
thing possibly be me?

Father, I can see
how every temptation is
    essentially the same:
to be so consumed by the need
    to fill and fulfill
myself, that I forget that it is
    your life that fills
mine; and all I need
    is to turn my face
  for the blessing
and then sit down to the food
    with which you grace my table:
always more than
enough for the day.   Amen.

May 21
Ascension of the Lord

When he had said this, as they were watching, he was lifted up, and a cloud took him out of their sight.

(Acts 1:9)

Lord Jesus—you came
    promising friendship.
There are many words
by which you call
      us, but there are days
      like today
I need to hear you
    call me *friend*.

Today we remember how
you departed from your friends
      and from the earth
altogether—to be
with the Father who,
    by leaving, you
    never left.
And when you left
    your friends
there on the mountain
      you told them that
      you had to leave
so that you might always be
      with them; so that
they might, like
fledglings pushed
    from the nest, either
believe and
    fly, or

fall.

Lord, I think of Peter
who, not long after you left
      him with the others, found
      to his wonder
and joy, power to stand
    on his own and
speak—and that the words
which came from his mouth were
      not his words but
your word—and yet
      the words were his.

Peter grew up
that day from a student
      hanging, at your feet, on
your every word, into
      an apostle
who found himself
      finding he could stand
alone and speak, confident
you were with him though
      you were with him
no longer.

So yes—I think
I understand, Lord, why
      you must leave us
so that you can be more completely
    with us. I think
I understand, Lord, why
      it's only by your absence
that you create
space enough for me to be
myself, to stand and
      to speak.
I think I understand, Lord, that

you call your people to be
        birds of faith
and for that we cannot
        always be cheeping in the safe
nest of your presence—but must be
        pushed out where
there is nothing
        to hold onto, nothing
solid to stand on, nothing
        but thin air to
keep us from falling.

But it is hard, Lord,
always to be
        pushed away.
It is hard always to be
        made to test
our wings against the air
        of your absence.
I think I understand, Lord, why
you must leave us in order to
        be with us. But,
        like having to die,
understanding that something is
        necessary doesn't always
make it less hard.

Growing up is hard, especially
        when I so often
        feel bewildered
        by the world, as if
I'm the only child in a room
        full of grown-ups.
But then I hear you say,
        suffer the children.
I hear you say, *you are*
        my friend—
and even though I still can't

>   touch you, the air suddenly
> is more solid than ground, and
>   your word makes my heart
> brave.   Amen.

May 22
Easter Feria

So you have pain now; but I will see you again, and your hearts will rejoice, and no one will take your joy from you. . . . Very truly, I tell you, if you ask anything of the Father in my name, he will give it to you.

(John 16:22–23)

Our Father in heaven,
>	*deliver us from evil.*

When my heart goes
out to you, Father, when
>	I turn to you
for deliverance; when I am
needing assurance that I am
>	held, that I am
saved, what am I asking for?
What do I believe
>	I'm praying for? Less,
I confess, something I imagine
>	I need to be delivered *from*
>	and more something
I obscurely desire
>	to be delivered
>	*into*—a new life, clear
as day, intimate as plainsong,
in which I see and hear and
>	know you are
everywhere I turn.

But I'm afraid, Father,
that this prayer comes
with a cost that I don't know
>	how, or that I'm

    prevented from, or that
I'm simply reluctant
   to pay: the cost
of trust; of hoping for nothing
    but love's store; the cost
of giving myself to you as completely
     as water gives
      itself to the run
of the river . . .

Holy Father, what prevents
me from trusting
myself this completely to
    your time and your provision?
What prevents me from joyfully
trusting your son's commandment to take
    nothing for the journey:
   no bread, no bag, no
  money in my belt?

It's not because he wants
to deprive me that he says
these things. It's rather to
    teach me what love is,
    what trust costs and
that hope against hope which
    the world cannot give.
Jesus says these things to me
because I have asked
    to know you, Father;
because I have asked to understand how
    to sing in unison;
how to pour myself out
    with the run of the River.

Is it evil
preventing me from knowing
    you with the intimacy

I believe I desire?
Or do I only imagine
    you've given me more
capacity for truth
    than I in truth possess?
Is my prayer a kind of false-pride?
Does it betray the shallows
    of my faith?

Father, forgive me. I often feel so
    dammed up—as if
something holds back the waters
    of my life so that
      only a trickle meanders
    through, while the great mass
of the water churns over and
    over on itself, waiting
    for a shift in my soul,
for the hour I no longer keep
    back from trusting entirely my life
    to yours.

Father, is it evil that dams
up the life in me and
prevents me from knowing you
    with that depth of trust
that I believe
    that I desire?
Is this evil something
    in me—or does it come
from outside of me?
I am tempted, Father,
to believe evil is
    extraordinary and so ought
to be easy enough to spot.
Help me, Father, to be
    aware of all the ordinary
ways evil dams the water-

     courses of your life
in mine. Help me, Father,
        to learn with my whole being
how to pray
        deliver us from evil.
Help me, Father, to trust
        my life to yours, to pour
my life out, to pitch
        every note, holding nothing
back.   Amen.

May 25
Venerable Bede

God gives the desolate a home to live in;
    he leads out the prisoners to prosperity,
    but the rebellious live in a parched land.

(Psalm 68:6)

Heavenly Father,
I am trying not to be
anxious about things
over which I have no
    say. I've been trying, Lord
      to wait
for whatever it is
    the hour calls
for; I've been trying
    to wait
for whatever it is
    you have to say,
    and to trust
you will give me
whatever I might need when
    I need it.

But, Father, hours
and days come and
    go without clear
direction; without a plan or
    plain word from you—
unless, that is,
    this is your word: to wait
more prayerfully, more
fully expectant
    of nothing

          more than our daily
bread.

Still, Lord,
I find myself full
        of busy worries—even more now
that the cafes and shops
        are opening again.
I'm not worried for
my health, but I'm finding it
confusing, seeing how it goes now
        and knowing
        we won't be returning
home to our parish
        family at once and all
together: the table set, the thanksgiving
        feast laid out in
          celebration, but we will return
        at a trickle, as if
furtively, with masks on,
        forbidden
        even from singing . . . I don't know,
but when I imagine this, Lord,
this fragmentary home-coming,
        I confess that it grieves
me. And although I understand
        why it's necessary, I don't
understand, Lord, why it is
necessary.

There's so much talk and constant
speculation, but what
        I believe
I need, Lord,
        is quiet: the quiet,
as it were, before an intake
        of breath; quiet
enough to understand what

    is not for me
        to understand; quiet
enough to trust
even that grief also
        is a song of love and
of trust and that you're asking
        me to give
my grief and care into
        your care.

Each Sunday, Lord, on returning
        home from church, Jasmin and I
habitually reviewed the morning,
      remembering especially the people
who were there and the people
        who weren't. This was our way
of checking in, of expressing
our joy at seeing those who
        were present and our care
for those who were not. Father,
as the days of this shut-down drag
        on, I find I'm like a hen
whose chicks are scattered in
the undergrowth: she runs about
the yard, head cocked and blinking, not knowing
        how to gather them in.
    Or I'm like a mother who
        every night peeps in on each
of her sleeping children before
she turns in herself:
        she *knows*, of course, that
        they are fine
but she still needs to know that
        they are fine.

Help me, Father,
    to wait. For
what would faith *mean*, and

        what would trusting in you
mean, if not a life
        devoted to learning
how to *wait*: devoted
to learning how not to be
        always imposing our own impatient will
on the world, but how to pray
        your will be done
on earth
        as it is in heaven.   Amen.

May 26
Augustine of Canterbury

I have made your name known to those whom you gave me from the world. They were yours, and you gave them to me, and they have kept your word . . . and I have been glorified in them.

(JOHN 17:6, 10)

Lord Jesus, I am
sorry. Today I woke
up knowing I had failed
you; feeling such
a hypocrite. This morning
I began, but the words
      of my prayer—stones meant for
throwing far out into a deep
      ocean—were hollow
and merely floated in the shallows
      where
I tossed them . . .

Lord Jesus, you once said
in no uncertain words, *just as*
      you did it to the least
      of these . . . you did it to me.
Last night we received
a call from someone in
      distress, perhaps not an
      emergency, but—in any case,
someone I know, but—who
      lives
on an edge we don't live
on. He called, wanting or
      feeling he needed a safe
place for the night and

although I wasn't afraid,
        we didn't offer. We didn't
open our home to him.

I don't want to ask why.
There are likely a thousand
        prudent reasons, but
the plain fact is, we didn't—and
it was, after all, such a simple
thing, really. A little, or not so
        little, thing. Lord, you once made
it clear that *whoever is*
        faithful in a very little is
        faithful also in much—the
reverse being just
        as true. Last night we
discussed and decided, though
not in these words, that
        safety trumped
trustfulness, at least for
        the night. But this morning
I'm sure, Lord, that it was
        you we turned away from
        our door—you, the one
I pray every day will
        come and make
        your dwelling in our
house, we turned you away when
you knocked on our front door.

Perhaps I ought
to ask your forgiveness, now,
Lord. But something in me
      recoils from that.
Before asking *your*
forgiveness, I believe I need
        to ask for his.

I understand, Lord,
the need to feel that
one's home is one's "safe
        place," but we
sinned, I'm sure, by
permitting our need, maybe even
        our comfort? to over-
rule your one
        rule: *to love*
        your neighbor as yourself.
I'm sorry, Lord
        Jesus: sorry that we
failed you; sorry that we
failed to be your body for
        that man whom you love;
I'm sorry that I failed to live
        up to the image I cherish
of myself living as
a reflection of your
        image; sorry that
we failed, last night, to be
the church.

Lord, I believe you
never ask of us things
        we are not able
to give. Lord, forgive
        us and help us
to show that with you
        we are stronger than
we think.   Amen.

May 27
John Charles Roper

Sing to God, O kingdoms of the earth;
    sing praises to the Lord.
O rider in the heavens, the ancient heavens;
    listen, he sends out his voice, his mighty voice.

(Psalm 68:32–33)

Lord Jesus, Christ Jesus, I believe
that when I pray
    it is you, your Holy Spirit,
praying in me; that the words
    I speak to you
are the words
    you are speaking to me;
that when I am deep in
prayer, I am listening
    more than I am speaking;
receiving more than
    I am giving.

But, Lord, it seems certain
expectations have crept into
    my times of prayer. I have come
to expect a certain intimacy or
    reciprocity between us.
Even when my prayers express how
    lost I feel, my bewilderment as
to your whereabouts, or
acknowledgment of my failures
    of faith, I am
    still strangely comforted,
knowing it's your Spirit
    moving in my longing

   for you.

But lately I've noticed,
in my morning meditation,
a kind of impatience—boredom,
even, as if the same words which
   bore once such gifts are now
tired of the burden, and no longer
robust enough even to break
through the surface
   tension of my brain.

Where I liked to linger
   on every nuance of your every
word, I've grown impatient.
   I race to finish
and must consciously force myself
   to slow to a walking pace,
  a listening
pace. But, Lord, lately
that sense of your being
at the center of my
   prayer eludes me.

I have considered, Lord,
changing the *form* of
   my prayer, hoping that
   novelty might help.
But you have prevented
   me from that. If
through prayer you are teaching
   me how to pray, how
   to wait without
expectation; if you are
trying to wean me

            from requiring
                    constant gratification,
                constant re-assurance of our
intimacy, then how do I know
            this boredom isn't your answer,
            isn't your teaching
me to grow up
            in what I have, after all,
                asked for: how to
wait; what it means to
wait; what patience
    is, and how to trust.
In which case, the need for
            novelty is a temptation.

Lord, you know
            what I need before
I ask—and you sent me this
morning a word from one of your beautiful
saints, who reminded me that

> once we have grasped the true nature of prayer . . . if we are wanting God and not ourselves . . . (we) will always know what to do and never be thrown by what (we) feel or don't feel. . . . Asking nothing for myself—no feedback or assurances . . . I will persevere through thick and thin . . . I don't ask to see the gift in my hand, to feel I have passed through the open door and received the bliss of his embrace. All my concern is that God should have what he wants: the chance to be good to me to his heart's content. And this surpasses all my understanding.[7]

Thank you, Lord Jesus, for
knowing my needs before
        I know; for being
so patient with me when
I find it so hard to be
            patient with myself.

Thank you for answering
my prayer even when
I need you to teach me
    to trust it;
    how to wait and to
listen and to know
it is your word
        I hear.   Amen.

May 28
Easter Feria

I keep the Lord always before me . . .
Therefore my heart is glad and my soul rejoices;
 my body also rests secure.
For you do not give me up to Sheol,
 or let your faithful one see the Pit.
You show me the path of life.
 In your presence there is fullness of joy.

(Psalm 16:8–11)

Father in heaven, you watch
over all things, caring
 and urging, comforting and
chastising and
 encouraging us to walk with
you on the path of life.

The birds outside my
window seem this morning
 especially busy. They seem to be
flying hurriedly in straight
lines and with what looks to
 me like more than usual
intent. Perhaps some of them are
attending to young still in the nest?
I wonder if they ever really get
 tired. Tired, I mean, with
that kind of tiredness with which
 I get so tired
and see so many others
 get tired—so deeply tired that
it doesn't seem to matter
 the amount of sleep

   one manages, but

this fatigue must be about something
 else.

 Our cat sleeps a lot, but
I don't think I'd ever
  really call him *tired*.
There's a kind of tiredness I
observe in myself, Father, that
 has come with aging but which
has little to do with the perplexing
 host of new aches and pains and
 rather with an impatience
I didn't know before, Father.
I wasn't aware that I've been expecting
  always more from my life than my life
was ever going to
  deliver. The stress of having to
narrow expectations, to narrow
 them, in fact, all the way down
to the ground, acts on me as
  a fatigue which sleep seems only to
exacerbate.

I think I understand, Father, that this
  fatigue is anxiety: the sensation that
I'm trapped in straight lines,
in horizontals, that there is no
  escaping this narrow hallway, no way
out, no fresh column of air. But you,
 Father: you rescue me from
the suffocating confines of
 my life.

When I pray, when I give
  myself to you in Eucharist; when
I write (which you know for me

has always been prayer)—when
        I walk in the soundless
forest or sit in a boat in the middle of
        a lake silent except
for the odd fish splashing or bird whose
        voice is always yours—your
Spirit, Father, expands
        in my lungs. Your Spirit reminds my body
          how to breathe,
        to stop the panic
that comes from holding too long
onto my own breath; to breath
        out and to breath
in again. When at worship together with
your people—then especially—
        you open windows inside me,
you open doors and *my heart*
        is glad and my soul rejoices; and
        my body also rests secure.

Then, Holy Father—perhaps it
        is then that I most become
like the bird, like the lily,
        who never tire but are always
busy in the day you
        have given them,
      a day that is always
more than enough.

Father, it is when
you remind me that I am
        more than I am
for you are
    my heart and you are
        my lungs and the breath
      of my lungs—that I
receive oxygen, the element of hope
and renewed possibility. Then,

      I'm at peace
for although my life's promise
          daily narrows down to
nothing—in your word
          I have space
          and time to grow in every infinite
direction and I
          rest in you, my God
and my Salvation.   Amen.

May 29
Easter Feria

He said to him a third time, "Simon son of John, do you love me?" Peter felt hurt because he said to him the third time, "Do you love me?" And he said to him, "Lord, you know everything; you know that I love you." Jesus said to him, "Feed my sheep."

(John 21:17)

Lord Jesus, you know that
        I love you. The question
is, how does my life,
how does every corner of my life
        reflect, witness, declare
this, the confession that lives in the heart
        of my heart? Why doesn't all
          that I do and say, give
        and desire,
bless your holy name?

I can't defend myself,
        Lord. And in any case,
there is no need, for you
        know everything.
I can't pretend to be
anything more than
        I am—though I find, when
I begin to excavate, I can't
        get to the bottom
     even of myself.
I can't defend myself, Lord,
        but I wish I could
stand before you, I wish I could
say "everything I am I return

    in thanksgiving
     to you." I wish I could say
I love you that perfectly: so
     perfectly there'd no longer be
discernable separation
     between what is
    mine and yours.

I know, Lord, you give me all
that I have. Yet I also know—
    because life has taught
me—that whatever I don't
    return to you in thanksgiving
(and to die grudgingly is still to hold
    on tightly to what you give), whatever
I don't return to you
    I lose, in the end.
I know, Lord, because
    you have taught me,
that to give is to
receive and to receive
    is to give. But why,
then, if I know
these things, do I find it
    so hard to do them?

Lord Jesus, help me to be
    fair to myself. You give
each of us gifts—gifts
    we can choose either to hoard or
return in Eucharist to you and
receive again, prepared
    for resurrection. I know, Lord,
that I receive gifts in such
abundance that at times
    I am haunted by your
reminder that "to whom
  much has been given, much

        will be required."
But what is it, Lord,
        that you give me
        to give?
What is it, Lord, you
        require of me?

Lord Jesus, you know that
        I love you and I know you
          bless me
        with so many gifts, gifts I have
in common with others:
        of family and friends, sun and
the rain, food and shelter and
even wealth, an education,
health, a sense of wonder and
        joy in small things. But, Lord,
when you say, to me as to Peter,
        "Feed my sheep,"
I am troubled by what food
        you require me to feed them.
You are our food, our bread, our
life. What have I to give? There is so much
hunger in the world. What is it
        you are asking of me?
I have, so it seems, only my love for you
        to give. And that is so
broken, so imperfect, so
        unsatisfying. It kills me every time
I let someone down—and
        that is so often.

But that trouble, I see
now I put it into words, is the insistent
        voice of pride talking over
your voice, your
        word in me. For the one true gift I have
        to give and to witness

and declare and to rejoice in the giving is
not my love for you but
        your love for me, Lord Jesus.
How is it I keep forgetting to remember
        you and your love,
your cross,
        before my own?

Lord, you know everything.
        When I try to discern
the gift you call out of me—it's not
        one that appears on Paul's list.
It is the gift of seeking
      truth in the love that makes us
        vulnerable. It is not, Lord,
a very glamorous gift but it is—
        may I say this?—it is precious
to me because I believe it is precious
        to you: the gift through which you call me
to love you and to
feed your sheep, your children
        learning, with me,
how to be loved.   Amen.

June 1

The Visit of the Blessed Virgin Mary to Elizabeth

And Mary said,
>*"My soul magnifies the Lord,*
>*and my spirit rejoices in God my Savior,*
>*for he has looked with favor on the lowliness of his servant.*
>*Surely, from now on all generations will call be blessed;*
>*for the Mighty One has done great things for me,*
>*and holy is his name."*
>
>(Luke 1:46–49)

Heavenly Father, I woke
this morning with unexpected energy
    and brimming with gladness, as if the day
called me into it with unusual
    promise. I sang, this
morning, a song of spontaneous
thanksgiving—to find, when I opened
    my Bible, that my song
    joined the song of Mary
and Elizabeth. How
    beautiful, the love
of these two women and
    their joy
at finding you
    are the word
of their greeting—joy
at finding themselves
    sharing in the wonder
    of being
    expectant with child; joy
at finding themselves miraculously
    at the fulcrum of your
    story, your mercy

taking life in them and leaping
        for joy at the promise
of the life to come.

We cannot know, Father, all
        that is in store for
us. My prayer that you help me
        to trust myself to
your future is
also a work of your mercy.
        Mary sings
her hymn of amazement and
thanksgiving, even though the
        very thing that today
swells her heart and swells
        her belly will one day also
pierce her heart. But the future,
        whatever awaits her, cannot
        negate, cannot
make any less
        joyful, this, her hour
        of joy. That is, in itself,
Father, a reason for joy
        and a reason to give thanks
to you, for the grace
        to live
in the day you have given us
        to live.

So I thank you, Father,
        for this day and for
these moments of especially
        unexpected joy—moments when
joy swells up in us for no reason
    —except, perhaps, for
the early light and the soft green song
        of life in the trees:
moments which come

        surprisingly and go—
    the surprise, no doubt,
an aspect of the joy
        of every unexpected gift;
renewing our sense of
        belonging to the day,
          that the day is given to us
to delight in, to give thanks for,
to bless and enjoy.

Father, I pray that you
help me to set whatever
        priorities need to be
set and to meet with
energy the coming days.
Help me to know
what must be done today
    and what can wait.
This is surely a time of re-adjustment,
perhaps especially of our
        expectations.
Help me, Father, to leave it to
        you to calculate what we may
have lost and what we may
        have gained. Help me,
Father, to let go
of the need to see too far
        ahead; to rejoice
when you fill me
        with rejoicing and to grieve
when my hour comes
to grieve; to know
I can arrange only
the things I can see,
    and I can see
only such a little way
        ahead.

Help me, Father,
> to trust in your mercy:
the gift of this hour
and the new life coming this
> new day.   Amen.

June 2

Martyrs of Lyons: Blandina and Her Companions

Turn, O Lord! How long?
    Have compassion on your servants! . . .
Let the favor of the Lord our God be upon us,
    and prosper for us the work of our hands—
    O prosper the work of our hands!

(Psalm 90:13, 17)

Lord God, when reading
the Psalms, I find such a
    brave palette of
emotions, expressed out loud,
      without reservation. The writers
of those prayers knew
    there's no word
      or thought of our hearts, no emotion
or desire or secret
    hope which you don't
know already. That thought is
fearful and sobering: that you see
    more of me than I can see
      of myself; that even those parts
    of me which I keep carefully
      hidden—from neighbors and
friends, hidden from you; hidden
from myself—since to you even
    the darkness is light,
things I attempt to pack
    away in boxes
are, for you, spread
    out on the front lawn in
plain sunlight. The knowledge
    you see right

through every visible and
        invisible wall is
dread-making. But it's also
        liberating, grace-giving: knowing,
with the psalmist, that if we *can't*
        hide from you
then it's useless even to
        try. If, though we bury
ourselves in hell, even there
        you see right
through to us—then we are
        free not to have
to try to hide. If
        you know us through
and through, then we are
        free not to be afraid
even to know ourselves.

Nothing shocks you, Lord.
        We don't need to
pretend or repress or
        forget. Your light shines
into my darkness.
        You see right
        into gloomy basement corners
where frustration and aggression, lust
        and selfishness and pride obscure
and make a mess
        of the love
you seek out and call
        from me:
        as when I pray
for change but do not truly pray
        to *be* changed; as when I pray
for one thing but still desire
        another. Even when we cry
out, feeling lost and fearing
abandonment; even when,

          as desiccated in spirit
as an empty vetch
          pod, we cry "O prosper
the work of our hands"—nothing
          can shock you.
You permit us desolation and
          joy, bitterness and
hope and even violence compounded
          together; and promise us
and give us faith that you
          are coaxing something beautiful
out of the tangle and
          this mess.

Lord God, I am frustrated.
      Why are things so stuck? Why
aren't we moving—our wheels
          spinning? Yesterday,
from the bishop's office, we received a letter talking
only about more talking. But
I am sick, Lord, of all the talking!
Perhaps you are trying to
          teach me patience but
I'm growing less
patient every day!

Lord, you know how
          I worry.
All this protracted uncertainty,
all this not-knowing, weighs
on me: how am I to serve
          and how am I to care
and how am I to let go
          of serving and caring,
     trusting
your grace: that I am truly not
          the life-
line you have given to the people

you have given me
        to serve.

But you also know, Father, that
        I have selfish motives
too for wanting things to
        get a move on. I am
itching to get out
        of the city; itching to get
things settled so I can
        rest.

This thicket of feelings, Lord,
the tangled branches of my heart,
        I lay at your feet, not
knowing how to
        make a pathway through them
by myself.   Amen.

June 3
The Martyrs of Uganda

And as for the dead being raised, have you not read the book of Moses, in the story about the bush, how God said to him, "I am the God of Abraham, the God of Isaac, and the God of Jacob?" He is God not of the dead, but of the living.

(MARK 12:26–27)

I believe in you,
my God, my Father.
I believe that wherever
      I am—you are there
also. When I find myself
      far from you—
days I can't remember
      my need for you; days
I shrink into the world;
      days I despair
at the destruction of so much
      that I love and that I know
therefore ties my life
      to yours, days I see nothing
but no end to the destruction,
      and wonder how you can possibly
leave us in this way
      to our own devices; or
times when, even as a pastor, I
am silenced in the face
      of another's suffering,
      unable to answer
or to hear you
      answer the question "why?";
even when I see no reason

        to hope; when I wonder
how any word you might have for us
        could possibly get through
so much chatter, so much "news," so
        astounding a proliferation of meaningless
words—I still believe in you,
        my God.

        I still trust, Father,
that if you are reticent,
yours is the reticence of
        love, bearing all
things. I still trust, Father,
that when you are silent,
yours is the silence of
        love, hoping all
things. Even when I knock
        and there is no answer, I trust,
Father, I trust that perhaps
        there just must be no answer,
at least of the kind I'm looking for
        and can accept as an "answer."
Therefore, the only answer possible
        is for you to ask of us
the patience of Abraham,
        the patience needed
            to stand long at cliff-edges
and so what it is,
Father, to trust in you
        alone.

My God, you create all things from
    nothing, so that even if, or
rather even *when* we fall—
        even if we take a step too far and
fall—you, my God,
        lift us up again; you
my God, return us to

firm ground again and
        restore us to life.

I believe in you, Father.
Although at every step I may be
        falling, you reach out
        to catch me.
Your hand is the earth
under my feet.
        And though days
and days sometimes pass when
you are present to me with
        no greater urgency than a
drifting thought or habit
of speech or routine
        gesture—yet, I can't
imagine life not set within
        exactly this
conversation, this prayer, this
        relationship which gives
substance to everything
        and which makes my life
real. Even your absence, Father,
        I experience as *your*
        absence.   Nothing
can replace it. My life,
from beginning to end,
        is a conversation
with you, though you do not
        speak to me in open words.
Yet I believe—believe
        that every word of mine is
a word by which you draw
me in and draw me further
        on . . . *into what?*
I cannot truthfully
say, Father, except further on
        in trust.

I believe in you, Father.
I believe in the promise
      you breathed into me when
you created me and gave me
life. I believe in the promise
      you breathe into me
each day, for each day
     you catch me, you raise
      the ashes of my life
through your word
that all this love and
      all this hope, this
body of mine—will not be
lost but gathered into
      your body: your
life pointing my life
      beyond my life—
to receive there, Father,
my life.   Amen.

June 8
Feria

I lift up my eyes to the hills—
    from where will my help come?
My help comes from the Lord,
    who made heaven and earth.

(Psalm 121:1–2)

Lord Jesus, it has been
a difficult week—and I
    need you to hear me.
You know, Lord,
that both Jasmin and I have
    dedicated ourselves to
your church and to
the people you have given us
    at St. Barnabas. All
our strengths and all
    our flaws we have
dedicated, and we have
lived by its joys and died
    by its troubles. Our
dreams have been
dreams of building, in
    this place and with
these people, a church,
    a household in Christ.
I believe that I've seen
glimpses of your kingdom, of
    your heavenly kingdom, of
        your promise catching the light
among us—but why, Lord,
    does it prove so hard to
sustain?

    Sometimes, I think
the problem must lie with
        me: that I must be trying too
insistently to hammer a
            square peg into the proverbial
round hole: that
          what I dream of just
isn't what a parish church is
for. But what, Lord—what then *is* it for?
      Where is the church if
it isn't also here? If it doesn't also
          begin here, with us,
            then in truth it begins
nowhere. Am I mistaken
        in this thought?

Lord Jesus, you have made me
a priest of your church.
To say that I'm "happy" in
          this calling would be like
saying I am happy
     having arms, a brain, a set
         of lungs: I can't
imagine how my life could be
          without it, for this is
how you have made me.
    How can I be otherwise,
therefore,
           than grateful? But, Lord—
hear me! Do I expect
too much? Of myself, but
do I expect too much especially
         of others—as if it's too
much to hope that the faith
you call each one of your children
        to live will, like the sea
to a fisherman, incline

>   all their dreams and be
> the bright
>   concern of every day?
> Are you not our God? Are we
>   not your people? No
> doubt I am putting this all
> much too starkly, but, Lord,
>   what would you have me do
> with all the love you have
>   given me? What would you
> have me do with all
> the hope you have
>   sown in me—dreams of sharing
> a life with those you have
> granted me, of devotion
>   to learning how to love
> you in each other—
>   a shared life where wants and
> needs are shaped not first
>   by our own wants
> and needs but by your demand
> we "love one another
>   as I have love you"?
>
> Lord Jesus, you know I'm not
>   judging. I'm only
> asking you to hear me.
>   Teach me how and teach me
> what to dream. Perhaps I ought
>   to learn to hold more lightly to
> people and things, as some
> advise. But that cloth seems too flimsy
> to fit me; too flimsy by far
>   to fit the love that takes you
>   all the way
> to the cross.

Hear me, Lord Jesus.
Help me to bear
.....disappointment. Interpret
my dreams to me; pluck out
.....the true
from the half-true and
the false.....Amen.

June 9
Columba of Iona

[The widow] went and did as Elijah said, so that she as well as he and her household ate for many days. The jar of meal was not emptied, neither did the jug of oil fail, according to the word of the Lord that he spoke by Elijah.

(1 Kings 17:15–16)

Lord Jesus, Christ
Jesus, wherever we find
ourselves, wherever we
      go, you have gone
        there already to wait
for us and to greet us when
      we finally arrive.

This morning, Lord, the sky
hung, heavy and
      dark, with pent up
rain—rain which you are
just now letting go of, opening
your hand and letting go of,
      in torrents.
The rain, Lord, seems
good. Even though
      I fear for my peonies. Just
the sound of it, the rain falling
in waves on the roof, is
    quieting and somehow soul-
making, cleansing.

This morning
I got out of bed reluctantly
and sat in the dark
      silence, for a while.

Then, Lord, you took
  pity, perhaps, and gave
me something: a sudden
moment of insight into
the suffering
  you suffered on the cross.
The moment came and
almost went and even
  now is fading as a dream fades
when you attempt to talk
  about it at the breakfast table
  in the morning.
I can't seem to hang on
  to it, but I pray, Lord, that
you gave me from
  your Spirit a seed
which will grow, perhaps
in time and as the
  rain, Lord, your
rain softens the tight
soil of—I believe the only
  name I have to give to
it is—grief.

Lord Jesus, I pray for all
  who are grieving.
I pray for all who, looking
ahead, see they've much
  more to lose than
to gain. Send them
  rain, Lord Jesus—rain
from your hand. Let them
  grieve, Lord Jesus, without
losing sight
  of the hope that you
  alone make
possible—hope that is, on
  the other side

of every humanly possible
        hope.

This morning,
        under dark clouds, you gave
us to read the story of
        the widow who you sent
to feed Elijah. The widow herself
had nothing left: her jar of
      flour was all but empty and
        she had no hope
        of filling it
again. Elijah found her
        gathering firewood
to bake her last meal—
        her last ounce of hope
for herself and her son. And when
Elijah asked, she shared
        even that last ounce of her life
with him, Lord, a stranger, just
because he asked and
because she saw that he was
        also starving, that he was
also without means or prospects
        or horizon beckoning him to
           step into the world. So
she shared with him her last
meal and, in sharing, found
        the flour in her jar
        did not empty. Every
day for many days, the
widow fed Elijah, shared
        with Elijah the last
handful of flour she
scraped from the bottom of
        her jar. And every
morning, when she went
back, she found that, somehow, there

    was enough for another
day. Though she came again and
    again to the end, there was
always enough yet again
    in her jar to share and
to live.
    For many dry
days, it went on
that way until you, Lord,
    at last sent
the rain.

Help me, Lord Jesus, to have
faith like the widow's
    faith. May you cause
even this prayer to restore
    hope again
in its sharing. Amen.

June 10
Feria

I bless the Lord who gives me counsel;
*　　in the night also my heart instructs me.*
I keep the Lord always before me;
*　　because he is at my right hand, I shall not be moved.*

(Psalm 6:7–8)

I believe in one
　　　Lord Jesus
Christ: God, of God; Light,
　　　of Light; very
God. I believe that when
I walk in patience, when
　　　I listen
with attentiveness to the movements
　　　of my inmost
heart, when I quietly
approach the lake-
　　　edge of my soul, nearing
the mysteries that hunt
　　　over the surface of my life—
then I believe,
　　　Lord,
you bring peace when I am in need
of peace; strength to persevere when
　　　I need to persevere; words
when I am in need
　　　of words; joy (or
that welling up of gratitude
　　　and fullness of heart
which I call "joy") on those days
　　　when I am
　　　at sea.

I remember, Lord, one particularly
difficult season, a season in which
        I really had no idea why
there was so much
        upset and trouble boiling
around me. I needed to do a lot
of walking, then. And wherever
I walked, I sang *Glory*
        be to God on high; and
        in earth peace, goodwill towards
        Men. Over and
over I sang the *Gloria*
        aloud, clinging
to its melody, pacing
myself to
        the rhythm of its praise—for I felt
        it was through this
music, these words, that
        you clung on
to *me*, held me up-
right, kept me from
        slipping until the ground finally
steadied and we found
a way through.

Yesterday evening, almost at
        dusk, we put out
in the canoe—to talk, but
really to listen for
        your word in the Swainson's
thrush, and in the flight of
        the day's last swallows, and
in the first swooping
        nighthawks; to allow
your word to speak
        to us through them and
through the softness of the

       air after the rain and
the slowly settling
           light. It's not, Lord, that
I believe you arrange
the world's weather patterns
to meet our individual needs, but
           I believe that when we
listen, you speak the word
           we need for the moment
           to hear. Things
have a way of requiring
time and peace to settle.
Resolution very seldom comes
           all of a-piece. And so, like
Abraham and Sarah; like Moses
           and Aaron; like Job—what can
we do, Lord, but wait and
           listen, walk and sing? For
I believe, Lord Jesus, I believe
because you have shown
           me again that it's at those
times when I wonder
           where you have gone,
wonder why you are not
           with me, that you have been
coaxing me into deeper
           water, waiting for me
there: waiting for
           me to let go of whatever
of myself I cling
           to for dear
life; waiting for me
           to wait and to
listen and to cling
           alone to you.

Lord God, Lamb
        of God: may this
prayer be the way you
have given me, today,
        to wait. May it be
the way you have given
        me, today, to listen. May it
be the song in which I
        hear you and through which you
grant us your peace.   Amen.

June 11
Corpus Christi

Remember the long way that the Lord your God has led you these forty years in the wilderness. . . . He humbled you by letting you hunger, then by feeding you with manna, with which neither you nor your ancestors were acquainted, in order to make you understand that one does not live by bread alone, but by every word that comes from the mouth of the Lord.

(Deuteronomy 8:2–3)

Lord Jesus, today is
Corpus Christi: the feast by which
    your church celebrates
the gift of your body
        and your blood, the gift
of the food we need to
        sustain us in the hope
of our faith and to sustain
    us in the life
    of your body.

In more usual days, we
would have gathered to
        celebrate the day
with a service of
    Solemn Evensong with
            Benediction. But today
we must find a way
to celebrate precisely what we
        find ourselves unable
to celebrate. It is
strange, Lord, to say thanks for
a gift we are unable
        to receive; it is

strange to say grace for
a meal when we are barred from
coming to the table.

We are your people, Lord, living
in exile from the very
   thing that makes us your
people. We are your
  people driven into
this desert. Whether it was you,
Lord, or some other power that
brought us to this
   place, I really don't
know, and in a sense I'm
not sure it matters. I believe
   what matters is to find
that whether in the desert or
   at the farthest limits of
   the sea; whether we ascend
   to heaven or make our
   bed in Sheol, you are there.

"... in the same night that
he was betrayed, our Lord Jesus
Christ took bread; and when he
had given thanks, he brake it; and
gave it to his disciples, saying
'take, eat; this is my
Body which is given for you: Do
this in remembrance of me.'"

Lord Jesus, who was it
   that sent you, that night, into that exile?
Who was it that sent
you, Lord, into the desolation
   of *that* desert? Was it really
your Father, or was it some
other power? If the latter, then

         did your Father and our
Father make a deal
      with the devil—a deal
with the darkness—knowing as
   he did so something
we cannot know: that
even the deep
     darkness, Lord, in
       your hand is a trick
of the light.

We have been sent into
       this desert, Lord, where we find
ourselves banished from your
table, where there is no
food for us—and yet we have found
     food for us, here.
So we lift up, Lord,
our voice in thanksgiving
      to you, for even if it wasn't
you who led us out into
     this desert, you have
nevertheless followed us all
     the way here. You have
fed us and you sustain
us with unexpected
      food—food fit for
this hour of our exile, this
time of our wandering in
      uncertainty; food for which
we would not otherwise
even have known
   how to ask.

I see, Lord, the hunger in
    all those thousands of
people who have been
     marching in the streets

of the world: people thirsting and
        hungering for justice, for racial
justice—for the food, Lord,
      of your love in which every
difference disappears except the
essential difference: the beauty
      in each one which love
only can see and only
love can know. All those
thousands, Lord, are hungry
      for your body; they
are thirsty for your blood; they
are your people! Angry
      today at finding themselves
in a desert of flinty rock where
    water is scarce
        as the source of justice
          in the earth. Lord, come
      and feed your people; sustain us
with the food of your word; help us
to find the food that is
even in this desert.   Amen.

June 15
Feria

If anyone forces you to go one mile, go also the second mile.
(Matthew 5:41)

Father of our Lord Jesus
Christ, he who is
      our pattern of
        patience; our song
of goodness; our reckoning
      with truth: three days ago,
we were given the date on which
we again can gather
      as your body
        for worship.
That announcement shifts
      the shape of our life once
again. We're still walking
this desert road, though it seems
      the terrain is changing: the mood
of the landscape beginning
    to feel more spacious.
But I don't want to grow too
accustomed, Father, even to this
      more open place.
      We're still far from
home. I don't want, Father, with
our growing familiarity with
    plexiglass and face masks
      to slide unwarily, unprotestingly,
    into a world scarred
by the acne of fear.
That is *my* fear, Father: that
      fear divides us, is increasingly

accepted, made visible, and
called by such soothing names
        as "safety" or "well-being."
Perhaps the lesson you
        hope we learn in this shut-
down is how, despite all our
        pretences to the contrary,
despite our technologies and
        our safety protocols and
our tracking devices—how
        vulnerable we always
are. We are vulnerable,
Father, and so we are often
   afraid. And yet, you've
shown—on the cross
        of your Son—that
it is love which makes us
vulnerable. As every
        parent knows, Lord, love
and suffering go
together; and it is learning
        to love that makes us
        suffer. How can we see
the cross in any other
   light? Why else, Father, would
your children have to wander
        so long in the desert, if
it wasn't to help them learn
to be vulnerable and how
        to trust? Just because
you were their God and
        they your people did
not make them any less
        assailable or any less
subject to every fear and
        finitude of being
        human. Rather, we believe
it was to learn how to be

even *more* human that they
      had to wander; learning
         weakness as
the first lesson
      in what it means to be
         made in your image—a creature
made for the love that is
      the life of the world.

Father, I can't know, but
      it seems you are shifting
my attention suddenly now toward
new priorities, and bringing
      the time you've given me
over the past three months for
these prayers to an end.
      I had no idea,
Father, when you started me
      off on this work of writing
and sharing with others
      my private words
with you, just how far
you would take and stretch me. I've
      sought, Father, only to listen
as attentively and as honestly as
I could—and you have
      tested the tenacity of my ear and
the discipline of my
      heart and I'm amazed and so
thankful.

It seems, Father, that you've been
teaching me every day as
    I've prayed, how to
pray. Your servant Simone Weil
once wrote that prayer "is the
      orientation of all ones'
        attention toward God."[8]

I've offered these prayers,
        Father, first to you and then
to those who have walked side-by-
     side with me, believing you
hear and accept them as
what they are meant
        to be: offerings of
attentiveness and
        Eucharist.

Father, bless us, your
people, your children, now
        as we are steered toward
another new way of striving to be
        your church. Help us to
meet every new day with
praise and thanksgiving and to find
pathways to serve you in each
        other. Condition our bodies and
our minds in love's
        moment. Teach us in
everything that we think
        and do what it means
to pray. Amen

Endnotes

1. Brother Lawrence of the Resurrection, *The Practice of the Presence of God*, trans. Donald Attwater (Springfield, IL: Templegate, 1974), letter 16.

2. Ruth Burrows, *Essence of Prayer* (Mahwah, NJ: Paulist Press, 2006), 88–89.

3. St. Augustine, *Confessions*, trans. R.S. Pine-Coffin (Middlesex: Penguin Books, 1961), 231.

4. Julian of Norwich, *Revelations of Divine Love* (Middlesex: Penguin Books, 1973); William Blake, *Auguries of Innocence*.

5. Simone Weil, *Waiting for God*, trans., Emma Crauford (New York: HarperPerennial, 1973). T. S. Eliot, *"Four Quartets*, "East Coker" (New York: Harcourt Brace Jovanovich, 1971), 28; St. John of the Cross, *The Ascent of Mt. Carmel*, 1.13.11 *The Collected Works of St. John of the Cross* (trans. Kieran Kavanaugh, ICS Publications, 2010).

6. St. Augustine, *Confessions*, trans. R. S. Pine-Coffin (New York: Penguin Books, 1961), 21

7. Ruth Burrows, *The Essence of Prayer* (London: Burns & Oates, 2006), 41.

8. Simone Weil, *Waiting for God*, trans., Emma Crauford (New York: HarperPerennial, 1973).

www.ingramcontent.com/pod-product-compliance
Lightning Source LLC
Chambersburg PA
CBHW051052160426
43193CB00010B/1154